Short Scripts
for
Puppet Plays

By Rod Spence

Illustrated by Craig Boldman

STANDARD PUBLISHING

Cincinnati, Ohio   14-03327

Second Printing, 1989

LIBRARY OF CONGRESS
Library of Congress Cataloging-in-Publication Data

Spence, Rod.
  Short scripts for puppet plays by Rod Spence.
    p. cm.
  Summary: Seventy-six very short scripts, many based on contemporary television characters, with a moral lesson or Biblical application. An introduction includes basic information on starting a puppet ministry, directions for building a
stage, and information on music and copyright.
  ISBN 0-87403-481-7
  1. Puppets and puppet-plays in Christian education.
[1. Christian life—Drama.   2. Puppet plays.]   I. Title.
BV1535.9.P8S64 1988   87-32921
246'.7—dc19   CIP
                                                                 AC

Introduction

The scripts you are about to read have been developed over the past decade and used across the country for both television and live productions. They are contemporary in nature—often naming current events, famous people, spoofs of popular shows, and so on. Therefore, these scripts contain many different types of characters. I've found that by using current names and fads that the children are "into," I instantly have their rapt attention. These scripts, if necessary, can be easily updated—usually by the substitution of a new name or changing a couple of words.

Most of the scripts are simple productions requiring no more than two or three puppets. I would suggest that, if you have the capability, you insert music both at the beginning and ending of each skit as you produce it so that the children will know when the skit has ended.

I like to begin my skits with a patriotic march and end them with a little jingle (see the resource guide at the end of this book).

Finally, everything you do in puppetry, do it as unto the Lord. Remember, we're in competition with the world, and the world doesn't compromise in the area of quality. The only difference between a professional and an amateur is *attitude*. If you have a professional attitude, and seek to do your best with what God has given you, then you'll be a professional.

May God bless in your efforts, which will pay you eternal dividends.

Table of Contents

A Few Words
About Your Puppet Ministry

Having an idea is easy. Setting it into motion requires a little more effort, but the most difficult part is carrying an idea full term and actually bringing it to a life of its own.

As a traveling puppeteer, I've visited many churches that have puppets of their own gathering dust in a closet somewhere. Someone in each of those churches conceived the idea of using puppets, purchased a few, put on several shows, and then let the ministry die. Perhaps they didn't have enough dedicated workers to make a go of it, perhaps the work was harder than they thought it would be, perhaps they never really had the vision of what a puppet ministry can be and do; how it can bless the church (both children and adults), and the community.

Why Puppets?

Like it or not, when trying to capture attention, the church must compete with all the alluring glitter and mammoth productions of the world. I've noticed more and more cartoons being shown on Sunday morning TV—full of slam-bang action, thrilling adventure, fast music, sophisticated sound effects, and tie-ins with toys, books, and games. Why would children want to come to a boring Sunday-school class and listen to a boring lesson when the world offers such exciting alternatives?

Studies document that in non-illustrative lecture or teaching situations, students remember only two to ten percent of what is said. Teachers in church *must* teach in a vigorous, interesting, and exciting manner. One way to expand the horizons of your teaching is through puppetry. As an audiovisual tool, a puppet greatly increases the attention span and memory of your children. One time, a little girl came up to me and started quoting the lines of a puppet skit I'd put on a year before!

When using a puppet, you're no longer just a teacher, you're a storyteller. As such, you may use some of the very techniques used by Jesus to deliver a message straight into the human heart. Jesus knew that when a person ponders a story, its meaning will take root in the heart, where truth can bloom and grow.

Puppetry is an art form thousands of years old—not "kid's stuff"! To declare yourself a puppeteer in Europe, the Orient, and many other parts of the world, would earn you instant respect and veneration. And puppetry has always been in the church. The term marionette—a string puppet—literally means "Little Mary," referring to the puppet shows given in the churches of the Middle Ages.

The puppetry traditions of the United States are fairly new—mainly because we're a young country. Puppetry has flourished on television thanks to shows like "Kukla, Fran, and Ollie," "The Muppet Show," and "Sesame Street." And it is now enjoying a renaissance in churches across the country. As a result, the need for traveling puppet teams for vacation Bible schools, carnivals, and other community events is enormous. It's an area of ministry that is wide open and waiting for dedicated people to fill.

The Art of Puppet Manipulation

The key to good puppet manipulation is to make the puppet look as close to being a real person as possible. Never have a puppet standing still. A puppet without movement looks like a dead, inanimate object. Little, subtle movements—turning a head, looking around, a nod—make a puppet come alive. However, too much movement should be avoided. Don't be hyper; be real—unless the script calls for hyper-activity and exaggeration.

Keep your puppet's mouth closed unless you're speaking—don't let it hang open.

Keep your puppet's head looking downward, since that's where your audience is most likely to be.

Keep your puppet raised up—don't sink down as time goes by and your arm gets tired.

Enter and exit with walking movements—not like you've been shot out of a cannon or just fallen through a trap door!

Attach rods to the arms of your puppets whenever possible, since moving arms add a wonderful, lifelike quality. Rods can be made of coathanger wire, wooden dowels, or any other rigid material.

Selecting Puppeteers

I strongly recommend using young people in your puppet ministry—they love it! And, involvement in such a ministry is a great way to bring shy, introverted children out of their shell, and boost their self-esteem. Becoming a part of life's highest mission, the Great Commission, will hopefully inspire them to continue to reach out to their fellow man with the gospel as they grow into adulthood.

The Puppet Stage

Ten years ago, I designed my first puppet stage. It was a masterpiece—a glorious puppet castle eight feet high, twelve feet across, and six feet deep. Unfortunately, it took several people almost thirty minutes to put it together, it weighed slightly more than a Sherman tank, and was too big for most small churches!

Since then, each new stage has been simpler and weighed less than the one before it. Stages shouldn't be too elaborate anyway—it detracts from the puppets. The puppets should always be the central focus. Enhance the puppets, not the stage. Avoid flashy curtains and exotic designs. And use only props that pertain to your story.

There are two basic kinds of puppet stages: the proscenium stage—with an opening in the front where puppets can come through—and the kind of stage where the puppets merely appear over the top. I've found the latter to be the simplest. What's best for you really depends on your purposes for the show. A puppet can always peek through a door, out from under a table, or even from inside a large cardboard box. But if you want a professional look to your show, then build an appropriate stage.

The following diagram shows you how to build what I believe is the best, most economical, and simplest puppet stage you can build. The section in Figure 1 is built with wood 2x2's. Each corner has an angle bracket attaching the 2x2's together. Use wood screws to attach the angle brackets.

The height of the section should be determined by the height of your puppeteers, and whether you want them standing, kneeling, or

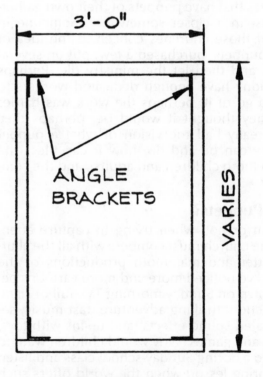

FIGURE 1

sitting as they work their puppets. I've put the width of the section at three feet. This makes each section very portable—easily fitting into vans, station wagons, and most cars.

At least two sections are needed to hold the stage upright. Simply attach the sections together with a short piece of rope at the top and bottom of each section (Figure 2). You can make as many sections as you wish, making the stage as long as you want it. You can even make it into a circle.

The easiest way to drape a curtain on the stage is to make it long enough to throw evenly on both sides (Figure 3). Make it of wrinkle-and-lint-resistant material that is thick enough to keep light from penetrating it. Several times in the past I've run into problems with a light shining behind us, or sunlight streaming in through a window, as we were giving a show.

Sound Equipment and Special Effects

The type of show you want to produce will determine the type of lighting and sound equipment you will need. In a standard Sunday school situation, you may want your puppeteers to simply read from a script, or improvise and talk to the children individually.

Putting your script on tape allows you to add music and sound effects to your show. You can record and play your skit on a small tape player, or get your church's sound engineer to record it on the church's soundboard/mixer.

The bigger the show you plan, the better your sound needs to be.

Having your puppets lip-sync a popular Christian song adds a wonderful dimension to any show. You can legally play any record or tape during a public performance, but you *must not* make a copy of it or duplicate it in any way—or you'll be in violation of national copyright laws. If you wish to copy the music or sound effects onto the master tape of your show, you must get permission from the record or tape publisher—who may require the payment of a licensing fee (sometimes called a "needle-drop" fee). Another option is using non-copyrighted music for your show. Check the resource guide at the back of this book for a listing of places where you can obtain non-copyrighted music and sound effects.

Special lighting, especially when you're giving a show in a large auditorium or church, is useful to help focus attention on your show. Children are easily distracted by the things around them. A simple spotlight is very helpful in focusing attention. For other special lighting techiques, check stagecraft books at your local library.

And now, on with the show!

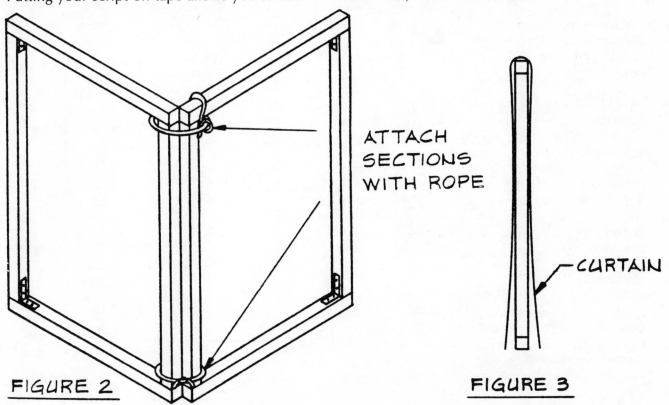

ATTACH SECTIONS WITH ROPE

CURTAIN

FIGURE 2

FIGURE 3

1.

The Toy Store

(*Sally and her dad enter.*)

Sally (*excitedly looking around*): Oh, Daddy! I want one these! And one of those! And this over here! And that over there! Please, Daddy, can I have them? Please?

DAD: Sally, control yourself!

SALLY: Oh, Daddy, look! Look over there!

DAD: Over where?

SALLY: Right over there! It's a real, live Sauerkraut Kid doll; Oh, Daddy, I've got to have one! Please?

DAD: You don't need a Sauerkraut Kid.

SALLY: But everybody has one! I'm the only kid in the whole world who doesn't have one!

DAD: Don't be silly, Sally—everybody doesn't have one.

SALLY: But everybody *I* know has one! Please, Daddy?

DAD: Sally, you're driving me crazy.

SALLY: I'll stop driving you crazy if you get me one, Daddy, I promise! And I'll keep my room clean, and wash the dishes forever and ever—if you'll just get me a Sauerkraut Kid.

DAD: You know how much those cost? Forty-five dollars! Forty-five dollars for the ugliest doll ever made!

SALLY: But you've got the money!

DAD: Sally, you're not getting a Sauerkraut Kid. That's one doll you can do without. You don't even play with the ones you have.

SALLY (*angry*): If you love me, you'll get it!

DAD: Well, young lady, is that a fact?

SALLY: That's right.

DAD: Well, starting tomorrow you're getting no more allowance.

SALLY (*shocked*): What?!

DAD: And you can start paying rent.

SALLY: What?!

DAD: And you can fix your own meals, buy your own clothes, and wash your own laundry.

SALLY: But, Daddy ...!

DAD: Because your mother and I must not love you anymore because we won't get you a Sauerkraut Kid.

SALLY: Oh, Daddy, stop being silly.

DAD: You're the one being silly. You know, I'd like to buy a few things too. I'd like to have a sportscar like Magnum P.I. drives.

SALLY: Then why don't you get one?

DAD: Because I can't afford it. I have a little girl to raise and put through school, a house to take care of, and taxes to pay. We don't always get what we want.

SALLY: We don't? Even when we get older?

DAD: Especially when we get older! Besides, the Bible says, "Thou shalt not covet." That's one of the Ten Commandments.

SALLY: What does "covet" mean?

DAD: That's desiring what someone else has instead of being satisfied with what *you* have. Grown-ups call it, "Keeping up with the Joneses."

SALLY: But we don't know any Joneses.

DAD: It's just a figure of speech. The point is, we should be thankful to God for what we *do* have—and to share what we have with others.

SALLY: I'd share a Sauerkraut Kid with my friends!

DAD: Would you really share it? Or boast about having one?

SALLY: Oh, Daddy . . . .

DAD: Look, you've got nice clothes, nice toys, all kinds of nice things—be thankful for what you *do* have.

SALLY: Are you thankful?

DAD: You bet! You know what I'm thankful for?

SALLY: What?

DAD: I'm thankful I've got you.

SALLY: Oh, Daddy ... And I'm thankful I've got you.

DAD: That's more like it.

SALLY: Oh, look! Over there!

DAD: What is it now?

SALLY: A Rambo doll! How about getting me one of those? A Rambo doll only costs *twenty-five* dollars!

DAD: Forget it—too violent. Besides, I'm not getting any doll that looks better than I do!

SALLY (*laughs*): Oh, Daddy!

(*Sally and her dad exit.*)

2.
The TV Kid

(*Dad is reading a newspaper. Sally enters*)

SALLY: Daddy! Daddy!

DAD: Not now, honey. Daddy's busy.

SALLY: Can I go swimmming today, Daddy?

DAD: We'll talk about it later.

SALLY: Please, Daddy, please? Can I go swimming? Can I? Can I? Will you take me? Please?

DAD: Sally, go away! Stop bothering me. I'm trying to read this. Go watch television or something.

SALLY: I sure wish you were like the daddy on television.

DAD: What daddy on television?

SALLY: The daddy on "Family Ties." He's a real wimp! He's easy to push around. The kids are in control on that show.

DAD: I wouldn't know—I've never seen that show.

SALLY: Television is great, isn't it, Daddy?

DAD: Best babysitter in the world.

SALLY: And very educational

DAD: That's right.

SALLY: TV has taught me all kinds of neat things, Daddy—like how to spike my hair and color it orange.

DAD: What?! Orange hair?!

SALLY: All the rock stars have weird colors in their hair on the MTV rock videos, Daddy. It's the in thing. Do you think Mommy will help me dye my hair orange?

DAD: No!

SALLY: But, Daddy—

DAD: I thought you were watching Sesame Street and learning your ABC's.

SALLY: I am. But I'm learning things from "MacGyver" too!

DAD: Like what?

SALLY: Like how to make a flame thrower from items you have around the house! I can't wait to try it! What a great show-and-tell it will make at school!

DAD: What else have you learned from television lately?

SALLY: I've learned how to lie, cheat, and steal from "Dynasty." How to wreck cars from "Miami Vice." And how to beat people up from "Simon and Simon."

DAD: Oh, no! I can see now I'm going to have to curb your television watching, young lady!

SALLY: I know! I'll just watch television when you watch!

DAD: That's a good idea.

SALLY: We'll watch ole J.R. together as he tricks Cliff out of his shares in West Star Oil.

DAD: What?!

SALLY: Well, that's your favorite show, isn't it?

DAD: Well, yes, but—

SALLY: And that Alexis on "Dynasty"—she's absolutely wicked, isn't she, Daddy? Hee-hee-hee....

DAD: I think we both need to revise our viewing habits.

SALLY: What do you mean, Daddy?

DAD: You know, it says in the Bible, "I will put no wicked or vain thing before my eyes." Vain means empty and worthless.

SALLY: Is television wicked and worthless?

DAD: Some of it is. But it can also be one of the greatest educational and informational devices ever invented. It can bring the world into your living room. But we need to use it wisely. And we also need to spend more time with it turned off.

SALLY: So we can have more time together. Right, Daddy?

DAD: Right!

SALLY: Daddy?

DAD: Yes, Sally?

SALLY: We could spend more time together if we went swimming.

DAD (*laughs*): Okay. Let's go.

SALLY: All right!

(*Sally and her dad exit.*)

3.
The Kingdom of God

(Sally and her dad enter.)

SALLY: Daddy! Daddy! Tell me a bedtime story! Please, Daddy, please!

DAD: All right. Which one?

SALLY: How about ... the story of Pistachio!

DAD: You mean ... Pinocchio?

SALLY: Yeah—that's the guy! Or better still, why don't you tell me a story I've never heard before?

DAD: What kind of story?

SALLY: One with kings and knights and dragons!

DAD: All right. Let's see .... Once upon a time there was a great kingdom that covered the whole earth. It was called the Kingdom of God. In this kingdom were many princes and princesses, but only one King—the Father God himself who reigns over the whole universe.

SALLY: Wow! This is better than *Star Wars!*

DAD: But there arose an evil prince named Satan who forsook the Kingdom of God and created his own kingdom called the Kingdom of Darkness.

SALLY: Boo! He's the bad guy, isn't he, Daddy?

DAD: That's right. And he set out to deceive the whole world, saying that there was no Kingdom of God. And he convinced many to serve him instead.

SALLY: But we know better, don't we?

DAD: Yes we do.... Now Satan sent out many lying dragons to deceive the world, but brave knights in the Kingdom of God rose up and went out to do battle with them.

SALLY: What were the knights like?

DAD: The knights were dressed in shining armor breastplates called righteousness, mighty shields called faith, and strong helmets called salvation. They carried sharp, two-edged swords called the Word of God. And they covered the earth, spreading the truth wherever they went, and capturing the enemies' strongholds.

SALLY: All right! Let's hear it for the good guys!

DAD: Now in this kingdom was a princess named Sally.

SALLY: Hey! That's me!

DAD: That's right. The only problem was, she didn't know she was a princess. No one ever told her.

SALLY: Imagine that.

DAD: You see, she listened to the lies of Satan that she was just a nobody, and that she would never amount to anything—when all along she was a princess!

SALLY: A princess in the Kingdom of God?

DAD: Right.

SALLY: But where is the Kingdom of God?

DAD: The Kingdom of God is in your heart—but also all around you. You see, when Jesus comes to live in your heart, He brings the Kingdom of God with Him, and He opens your eyes to the Kingdom of God all around you.

SALLY: I'm not sure I understand.

DAD: Sally, whenever you have peace and joy and you do what is right, that's the Kingdom of God working inside of you—because Jesus is sitting on the throne of your heart. And whenever you see God doing things around you—

SALLY: Like answering your prayers?

DAD: Right! That's the Kingdom of God working on the outside.

SALLY: Am I *really* a princess?

DAD: Yes you are. You're the daughter of the King, so that makes you a princess.

SALLY: Like Lady Diana and Cinderella?

DAD: The kingdom you live in is much greater than theirs.

SALLY: Wait a minute. If I'm a princess, why aren't we living in a palace?

DAD: One day we will—when the Lord returns to this earth from His throne in Heaven to destroy the Kingdom of Darkness once and for all. Then everyone will see and know the truth.

SALLY: And we'll live happily ever after—forever and ever. Isn't that right, Daddy?

DAD: That's right.

SALLY: I like that story! Because it's really real—not a fairy tale like Pistachio. Tell me another story.

DAD: Like what?

SALLY: How about . . . "Amy Grant and the Three Bears!"

DAD: You're silly, you know that?

SALLY: I know that.

DAD: Goodnight, Sally.

SALLY: Goodnight, Daddy.

(*Sally and her dad exit.*)

4.
What Is God Like?

(*Sally and her dad enter.*)

SALLY: Daddy dear, oh Daddy dear ...

DAD: Yes, Sally?

SALLY: I have a question, Daddy dear.

DAD: What is it, Sally?

SALLY: You're so smart, Daddy.

DAD: I know. I know.... So what question can your big, smart daddy answer for you?

SALLY: Daddy, what does God look like?

DAD: Well, I uh ... well, that's kind of hard to explain.

SALLY: But, Daddy, I thought you knew everything!

DAD: No, Sally, not *everything.*

SALLY: Hmmmmm. Daddy, do you at least know if God has eyes?

DAD: Well ... yes, God has eyes. It says in the Bible that His eyes run to and fro throughout the earth ... and that His eyes are always on His children ... and that He even sees every little sparrow.

SALLY: Hmmmmm. I wonder if God has ears.

DAD: Of course, because He hears our prayers. And He hears us when we praise Him, and sing songs to Him.

SALLY: What about a nose? Does God have a nose?

DAD: Yes. Because the Bible says that whenever we make a sacrifice to Him, that gift creates a sweet smell for Him.

SALLY: You mean a burnt sacrifice?

DAD: Whenever we give something to the Lord at our own expense, it's considered a sacrifice. But we must give our gifts to the Lord with a pure heart and the right motives.

SALLY: Daddy, does God have a brain?

DAD: Of course. He knows everything. He even knows the number of hairs on your head. And the names of all the stars in the sky.

SALLY: Does God have a heart?

DAD: Oh, yes. Because He loves us.

SALLY: What about hands? Does God have hands?

DAD: God's hands are the Holy Spirit. And with the Holy Spirit He is constantly molding and shaping us into something beautiful.

SALLY: Does God have ... legs and feet?

DAD: Well ... in the story of the Prodigal Son, when the son returned to his father—who represents our Father in Heaven—the Bible says that the father *ran* to meet his returning son. So, come to think of it, God must have legs and feet.

SALLY: Does God have arms?

DAD: God has strong, mighty arms! He is all-powerful. Just imagine the muscle God can make with His arms! And He keeps those strong arms wrapped around us.

SALLY: Does God have ... a mouth?

DAD: Yes indeed! God has spoken to mankind since the beginning. And He can speak to us today, if we'll take the time to listen for His voice in our hearts.

SALLY: Wow! It is beginning to sound like God is just like us!

DAD: Actually, we were made in *His* image. So we are like Him.

SALLY: Ohhhh.

DAD: You know what, Sally? The best way to see what God is really like is to look at Jesus. Because it says in the Bible that when you've seen and known Jesus, you've seen and known God himself .... You know what? I think I can picture God a little better now myself.

SALLY: So can I, Daddy. You're the smartest daddy in the whole world!

DAD: Well, it helps when you ask the right questions!

(*They laugh and exit.*)

5.
Sunday School

(*Billy and Tommy enter from opposite directions.*)

BILLY: Hi! My name's Billy. What's yours?

TOMMY: Tommy. Tommy Tyler.

BILLY: Glad to meet you. Is this your first time in Sunday school?

TOMMY: Yep. My very first time.

BILLY: Well, I hope you like it.

TOMMY: There's no way I'm going to like it!

BILLY: Why not?

TOMMY: Listen, I go to Monday school, Tuesday school, Wednesday school, Thursday school, and Friday school! So why do I have to go to Sunday school?

BILLY: You should give Sunday school a chance.

TOMMY: But I'm already suffering from an overdose of school. My little brain can only take in so much a week!

BILLY: But Sunday school is different from regular school.

TOMMY: What's so different about it?

BILLY: Well, you could call it *super* school.

TOMMY: Super school? What do they teach, anyway?

BILLY: They teach about everything! About life itself! You'll learn about history, geography, economics, psychology, sociology, health—all kinds of things. And God's Word, the Bible, is our textbook.

TOMMY: But they teach all those subjects at regular school.

BILLY: I know. But in regular school they leave out the most important subject—they leave out Jesus.

TOMMY: We study a lot of famous people at regular school. What's so important about Jesus?

BILLY: Jesus wasn't just another man. He was God's Son! And when He came to earth, it wasn't just to teach us *about* life, He came to show us *how* to live with His own life as an example.

TOMMY: Do you have recess in Sunday school?

BILLY: No, but Sunday school is only one hour a week!

TOMMY: I know. But recess is my best subject! What about homework?

BILLY: The homework is up to you. But hopefully, you'll like the Bible so much you'll begin to read and study it all the time.

TOMMY: Why should I?

BILLY: Ever hear of Larry Byrd?

TOMMY: Sure! The basketball superstar!

BILLY: Well, he didn't just walk out onto a basketball court one day and start winning games. He's practiced for years. Likewise, if you want to be a success in life, it's going to take hard work and discipline—and that includes studying the Bible on your own. Because if you follow what the Bible says, it will make you a champion.

TOMMY: Do you ever graduate from Sunday school?

BILLY: Never. It's a lifelong super school. Though one day you might want to be a Sunday-school teacher yourself.

TOMMY: Are you graded?

BILLY: Nope. The most important thing in Sunday school is that you try. If you really try, then you'll grow in knowledge and faith.

TOMMY: All right! No grades! In that case I might pass! What else does Sunday school offer?

BILLY: Fellowship with other Christians. It's important to have Christian friends, because a Christian friend can be a friend forever, and can help you stay close to the Lord.

TOMMY: Sunday school is beginning to sound pretty interesting. Maybe I'll give it a chance.

BILLY: And Sunday school is fun! We play games, have contests, and sometimes even refreshments.

TOMMY: Refreshments! All right! You know, I think regular school could learn something from Sunday school.

BILLY: So do I!

TOMMY: Well, let's get on with it! My little brain is ready to grow!

BILLY: All right! Let's go!

(*Billy and Tommy exit.*)

NOW PLAYING →

6. The Drop-Off Kid

(*Billy and Tommy enter from opposite sides.*)
BILLY: How you doing, Tommy?
TOMMY: I'm depressed.
BILLY: Why is that?
TOMMY: Just because....
BILLY: Well, there's got to be a reason.
TOMMY: It's too embarrassing to tell.
BILLY: Oh, come on! You can tell me. I'm your best friend.
TOMMY: Oh, all right. I'm depressed because ... because I'm a drop-off kid.
BILLY: A what?
TOMMY: A drop-off kid! Every Sunday my mom or dad drops me off at Sunday school—and then they leave! Then they pick me up after it's over, but they don't stay themselves.
BILLY: Well, I hate to admit this, but I'm a drop-off kid too.
TOMMY: You are? Really?
BILLY: Sure! There are lots of us in Sunday school.
TOMMY: Now I'm even more depressed.
BILLY: What excuses do your parents use?
BILLY: Have you heard the one about the TV preacher being just as good—so they stay home and watch him?
TOMMY: Yep. And sometimes my dad goes fishing on Sunday.
BILLY: Sometimes my dad and mom say it's their only day to relax.
TOMMY: Or they've got shopping to do.
BILLY: Or company is coming over.
TOMMY: Or they've got cooking to do.
BILLY: Or they don't want to dress up.
TOMMY: Or they haven't got nice enough clothes.
BILLY: Or the football game is coming on.
TOMMY: Or it's just too much trouble.
BILLY: Or the pews are too hard.
TOMMY: Or the preaching's too hard.
BILLY: Or the preaching's too long.
TOMMY: Or they'll come "one of these days."
BILLY: When they "get around to it."
TOMMY: It's amazing how many excuses they have. We ought to make a game out of this! And get the other drop-off kids involved.
BILLY: That's a great idea! What will we call it?
TOMMY: You've heard of "Trivial Pursuit"?

BILLY: Yeah.
TOMMY: How about calling our game "Trivial Reasons"?
BILLY: That's perfect!
TOMMY: You know, it's probably better to be dropped off than to not come at all.
BILLY: That's true.
TOMMY: But I've seen a lot of drop-off kids "drop out" when they get old enough and become just like their parents.
BILLY: Using the same excuses their parents used!
TOMMY: Maybe parents don't know that Sunday school is for adults too.
BILLY: Or maybe they just don't think it's important.
TOMMY: Then why should they expect *us* to think it's important?
BILLY: Or maybe they think that they know it all and don't have to come—except on Easter and Christmas, of course.
TOMMY: I don't think they know it all, because just last week in Sunday school we learned the scripture about how important it is to assemble together with other Christians at every opportunity since the Lord is coming back very soon.
BILLY: They must not know that scripture.
TOMMY: Or how about the scripture that says, "Train up a child in the way he should go, and when is is old, he will not depart from it"?
BILLY: I think drop-off parents think that Sunday school is supposed to do that.
TOMMY: You can't train a child to be Christian in just one hour a week.
BILLY: How much better it would be if our parents were good examples for us—so we could follow them!
TOMMY: Let's start working on them. And let's pray that the Lord will start working on them!
BILLY: I'm for that! Let's get to it! But where can we start?
TOMMY: I know! We can write a puppet skit about drop-off kids and then perform it for children and their parents.
BILLY: Tommy, I think we just did that.
TOMMY: Ohhhhh.
(*Billy and Tommy exit.*)

7.

The Christmas Story

(Tommy enters)

TOMMY: I'm bored. What a boring day. There's nothing on television and nothing to do.

(Suzanne, his sister, enters.)

SUZANNE: Hey, Tommy, hurry up and get ready for church or you'll be late.

TOMMY: But I don't want to go to church.

SUZANNE: Why not?

TOMMY: Because it's dull. And I'm already bored to death!

SUZANNE: But it's Christmastime! And they'll be telling the Christmas story today.

TOMMY: I've heard that story a hundred and fifty jillion times.

SUZANNE: So I guess you know everything there is to know about the Christmas story.

TOMMY: That's right.

SUZANNE: Then tell it to me.

TOMMY: What?

SUZANNE: Tell it to me!

TOMMY: I don't want to.

SUZANNE: Come on ... I'll bet you don't even know it!

TOMMY: I do so!

SUZANNE: Well ... ?

TOMMY: Oh ... all right. Once upon a time there was a good ole boy named ... ah ... Joe Duke.

SUZANNE: Joe Duke! You mean Joseph?

TOMMY: Now Joe Duke was engaged to his cousin Mary.

SUZANNE: What are you talking about?

TOMMY: Are you going to let me tell this story or not? Now an angel visited Mary and said, "You're going to have a son, and you'll call his name Jesus."

SUZANNE: At least you got that part right.

TOMMY: So then Joe and Mary got on their donkey—named the General Lee—and rode to a town in Nazzard County called Bethlehem. And that's where Jesus was born.

SUZANNE: Oh, brother.

TOMMY: Now most of Nazzard County was run by a mean ole king named ... Boss Herod.

SUZANNE: Boss Herod!

TOMMY: And Boss Herod was approached by three wise guys from the east.

SUZANNE: Wise *men*—not wise guys!

TOMMY: These wise guys wore turbins with gold tassels. And they said, "Behold, we are Hadi Shriners...."

SUZANNE: What?! They weren't Shriners!

TOMMY: Anyway, about this time an angel appeared to shepherds in the field tending their flock. The shepherds' names were Roscoe and Enos ...

SUZANNE: Stop it! Stop it! That's enough! How can you make fun of the Christmas story?

TOMMY: I'm just trying to liven up a story that's been told a hundred and fifty jillion times.

SUZANNE: That's all it is to you, isn't it? Just another story like the "Dukes of Hazzard" on television.

TOMMY: I suppose so.

SUZANNE: Tommy, this story really happened! It wasn't made up. God's Son was *really* born into the world ... You know what your problem is?

TOMMY: What?

SUZANNE: You just haven't *met* Jesus yet. Once you realize that Jesus is real, and that He's alive here and now, the Christmas story won't just be another story.

TOMMY: Maybe you're right.

SUZANNE: So let's get ready for church. And let's get ready to meet Jesus there.

TOMMY: All right. Let's go!

(Tommy and Suzanne exit.)

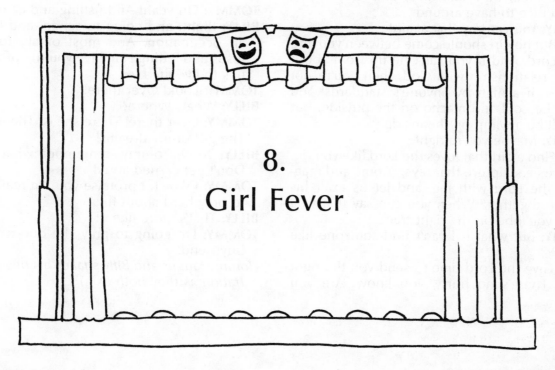

8.
Girl Fever

(Billy and Tommy enter.)

TOMMY: Billy, did you see that new girl in school yesterday?

BILLY: What girl?

TOMMY: What girl! If you'd seen her, you wouldn't be asking! Tall, slender, blond hair, green eyes—what a fox!

BILLY: Tommy, you shouldn't use language like that.

TOMMY: Like what?

BILLY: Calling a girl a fox! The only person Jesus ever called a "fox" was the evil King Herod.

TOMMY: All right then. She was a perfect "10"!

BILLY: And that's not very nice either. That's the world's system of grading girls.

TOMMY: But she was gorgeous! A real knock-out! Wait till you see her! Your eyeballs will pop right out of your head!

BILLY: But what do you know about this girl?

TOMMY: I know she's beautiful!

BILLY: But beauty is only skin deep. That's like a girl looking for a "hunk" or a "macho man"— all that physical stuff is only on the outside. It's what's on the *inside* that counts. A person can be handsome or beautiful on the outside, and totally empty or corrupt on the inside. They say that love is blind—so you better ask the Lord to open your eyes to true beauty.

TOMMY: But she's such a doll.

BILLY: You know what your problem is? You've got girl fever! Girls are all you ever think about!

TOMMY: They are not! Sometimes I think about *women!* Like Vanna White, Cybill Shepherd, and ... Vanna White!

BILLY: Let's see ... What do you think of ... Melba Groggins?

TOMMY: Melba Groggins! She's a flake! A real space cadet!

BILLY: I've got news for you—Jesus died for that so-called flake and space cadet! A person's real value is what's on the inside. Jesus looks on the heart! And so should you.

TOMMY: I don't care what you say—I'm going to ask that new girl out! I might as well get to know her.

BILLY: Where will you take her?

TOMMY: I was thinking about asking her to the skateboarding contest at the mall.

BILLY: What kind of place is that?

TOMMY: I want to show her I'm cool—that I'm really with it!

BILLY: Why don't you invite her to church?

TOMMY: What? And have her think I'm a religious fanatic?

BILLY: Listen, girls are nice. They look nice, they smell nice, they talk nice, and they're just plain nice to have around.

TOMMY: You can say that again!

BILLY: But no girl should come between you and the Lord. And if you can't be up front about your relationship with God, then you're not much of a man by anyone's standards! You may be cool and macho on the outside, but you'll be a wimp on the inside.

TOMMY: Maybe you're right.

BILLY: Find a girl that loves the Lord like you do. There's a scripture that says, "Come and magnify the Lord with me, and let us exalt his name together." When you can say that to a girl, you'll be on the right track.

TOMMY: But what if I can't find someone like that?

BILLY: Give the Lord time to send you the right girl! There's no hurry, you know. Are you trying to get married by your thirteenth birthday or something?

TOMMY: But what will I do in the meantime?

BILLY: There are other things in life besides girls.

TOMMY: There are? Really?

BILLY: Sure! There's softball, basketball, football—

TOMMY: Oh yeah! And fishing and camping!

BILLY: Right, and going to school and learning an occupation. And most of all, following Jesus and letting Him give you the proper values to live life by.

TOMMY: Look! Over there!

BILLY: What? Where?

TOMMY: Over there! There she is! The new girl! The girl of my dreams!

BILLY: Now, Tommy, remember what I said! Don't get carried away!

TOMMY: I won't. I promise you I'm really going to pray hard about this!

BILLY: That's more like it!

TOMMY: I'm going to pray she doesn't have a boyfriend!

(*Tommy laughs and Billy shakes his head in frustration as they both exit.*)

9.
Forgiveness

(*Billy and Tommy enter from opposite directions.*)

TOMMY: Boy, am I mad! I'm so mad I could bite through a nail!

BILLY: What's wrong, Tommy?

TOMMY: I'm red-hot, cinnamon-flavored angry! That's what's wrong!

BILLY: Who are you angry at?

TOMMY: Bigfoot Blansky! That's who!

BILLY: Who's that?

TOMMY: The biggest, baddest bully in school!

BILLY: What did he do to you?

TOMMY: First, he pushed me against my locker and knocked all the books out of my hands. Then he threw mashed potatoes in my face in the cafeteria. And then he made fun of me all day in class!

BILLY: That's pretty bad.

TOMMY: Why is he picking on me? I didn't do anything to him!

BILLY: Bullies like that don't need a reason – they just strike out at whoever's handy.

TOMMY: Well, I m going to get him back. You know the old saying, "Don't get mad – get even!"

BILLY: You don't want to do that.

TOMMY: Oh yes I do! I'd fight him, but he'd tear me apart. He's so tough he plays soccer with a bowling ball!

BILLY: That's tough all right.

TOMMY: I'll say it is. I wish I knew karate – I'd like to chop him down like a tree!

BILLY: That's not the answer.

TOMMY: You're right .... I know! I'll let the air out of his bicycle tires! That'll fix him.

BILLY: What good would that do? It would only make him meaner and madder.

TOMMY: You've got a point there. He's already mean enough.

BILLY: Do you really want to get him back? Really truly?

TOMMY: Yeah! You got an idea?

BILLY: Yes ....

TOMMY: Well, what is it?

BILLY: If you really want to get back at him ... then do something real nice for him.

TOMMY: What?!

BILLY: The Bible says help and bless your enemies. And do good to those who despitefully use you.

TOMMY: I guess that *would* freak him out. He'll wonder what I'm up to. Yeah! It will drive him crazy!

BILLY: That's not what you should hope for. Being kind to him would give you an opportunity to witness for Jesus when he asks you why you're being so nice. Who knows – it might turn him around!

TOMMY: Not Bigfoot Blansky!

BILLY: At least you could give it a try.

TOMMY: You really want me to be nice to him, don't you? You're serious about this.

BILLY: That's right.

TOMMY: But what about all that stuff he did to me?

BILLY: You've got to forgive him.

TOMMY: But why?

BILLY: Because the Bible says if we don't forgive others, then God can't forgive us. And also, by not forgiving, we're just making *ourselves* miserable. We let anger eat at us until we make ourselves sick. Besides, Jesus took all kinds of abuse without striking back. Shouldn't we follow His example?

TOMMY: I guess you're right. But it's so much easier to strike back.

BILLY: That's what the devil would tell you to do. But if you're going to find the peace and love of God in your life, you've got to follow the Lord's example. Let go of all that anger and you'll feel a lot better.

TOMMY: But what if, after being goody-goody to Bigfoot Blansky, he *still* pushes me around?

BILLY: Then we'll pray that the Lord will take care of things. He can deal with bullies like Bigfoot a whole lot better than we can.

TOMMY: Okay. I'll give it a try.

BILLY: That's the spirit! The Holy Spirit, that is. Let's go find Bigfoot and do something nice for him.

TOMMY (*laughs*): Okay, let's go!

(*Billy and Tommy exit.*)

10.
The Devil
Made Me Do It

(Billy and Tommy enter from opposite directions.)

TOMMY: Woe is me! Woe is me!

BILLY: What's wrong?

TOMMY: I'm in big trouble—that's what's wrong!

BILLY: Why is that?

TOMMY: I did something terrible! I've *really* done it this time.

BILLY: What did you do?

TOMMY: Friday at school I put a big wad of Bubble Yum bubble gum on my teacher's chair. And she sat in it! Boy, was Mrs. Huffnagel mad!

BILLY: Why did you do that?!

TOMMY: I don't know. It just seemed like a good thing to do at the time!

BILLY: But there must have been a reason.

TOMMY: All I can say is, the devil made me do it! Yeah, that must have been it! I'm a Christian, and I don't do things like that. So it must have been the devil!

BILLY: You mean that mean old devil made you buy that gum?

TOMMY: Well, no. I bought it because I wanted it.

BILLY: Oh. But the devil popped it into your mouth and moved your gums to chew it up real good?

TOMMY: No. I put it in there myself.

BILLY: I see. But the devil made you carefully plan when you were going to put the gum in the chair at just the right moment when nobody was looking?

TOMMY: Well, I sort of planned it out all by myself.

BILLY: Then the devil must have been right behind you, twisting your arm and forcing you to do it.

TOMMY: No, not exactly.

BILLY: Well then, when did the devil come into the picture?

TOMMY: I guess he didn't. I did it all by myself.

BILLY: Now the truth comes out!

TOMMY: Oh, why did I do it? I thought Christians weren't supposed to sin!

BILLY: Christians slip up and sin just like everybody else. We're not perfect, just forgiven ... You did ask the Lord to forgive you, didn't you?

TOMMY: Well, sure. I mean, I guess I did. I sure feel bad about it.

BILLY: Tommy, you've got to repent! Really repent of what you did! Not just feel bad about it.

TOMMY: What's the difference?

BILLY: Repentance means to turn around and head another way. It's a change of direction, a change of thinking about something. It means to ask forgiveness with the determination never to do the same thing again.

TOMMY: Oh ... well, sure ... I'll never do *that* again!

BILLY: Or anything like it.

TOMMY: Well....

BILLY: Tommy!

TOMMY: But don't you think it would be funny to put a snake in Mary's lunch box? You know how jumpy she is anyway!

BILLY: Can't you find something more constructive to do? Idle hands are the devil's tools, and idle minds are the devil's fools.

TOMMY: You're right. I'd better straighten up before I get into *worse* trouble.

BILLY: So what did Mrs. Huffnagel do to you?

TOMMY: Nothing.

BILLY: Nothing? Wow, she sure is forgiving.

TOMMY: She's not forgiving. She just never found out who did it!

BILLY: Tommy! You didn't confess?

TOMMY: Confess! Are you crazy? I'd be punished! The Lord has forgiven me—isn't that enough?

BILLY: God may have forgiven you, but you're still responsible for your sins against your fellow man—and teacher! If you're going to call yourself a Christian, you're going to have to be honest and 'fess up to Mrs. Huffnagel—and pay the price for your actions.

TOMMY: I guess if I'd followed the Lord to begin with, I wouldn't be in this mess.

BILLY: You'll know better next time.

TOMMY: If there *is* a next time. Mrs. Huffnagel might kill me.

BILLY: No, she won't. It's against the rules for a teacher to kill a student.

TOMMY: Are you sure?

BILLY: I'm positive.

TOMMY: I'm glad I don't have to tell her until Monday—that will give me time to pray! As it says in the Bible, "Yea, though I walk through the valley of the shadow of the principal's office, I will fear no evil, for thou art with me."

BILLY: Amen!

(*Billy and Tommy exit.*)

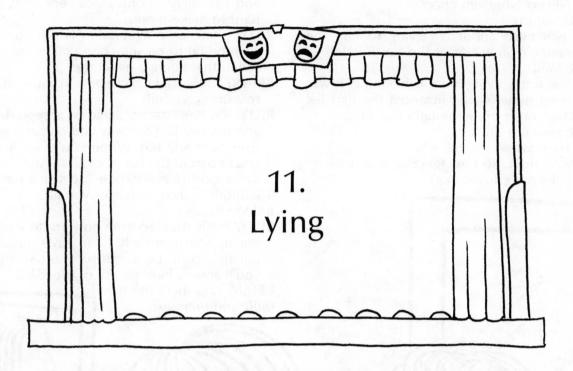

11.
Lying

(*Billy and Brian enter from opposite directions.*)

BILLY: Hello, my name's Billy. Are you new here? I don't remember seeing you in Sunday school before.

BRIAN: Yep. My family just moved into town.

BILLY: Really? From where?

BRIAN: From ... ah ... the North Pole.

BILLY: The North Pole! Really?

BRIAN: That's right!

BILLY: I didn't know people actually lived up there.

BRIAN: We did. My mom and dad are scientists. They were looking for the Abominable Snowman.

BILLY: You're kidding.

BRIAN: No! I'm serious!

BILLY: What's your name?

BRIAN: Brian. Brian Osterridge. *The* Brian Osterridge.

BILLY: *The* Brian Osterridge?

BRIAN: That's right. I was the spelling bee champion of the State of Wisconsin last year.

BILLY: Oh, you were originally from Wisconsin then.

BRIAN: No—I was raised most of my life in Africa.

BILLY: Africa?

BRIAN: Yeah. In Timbuktu. My parents and I would go on safaris and everything.

BILLY: Really? Really truly?

BRIAN: Yeah! I even had an orangutan as a baby-sitter.

BILLY: Oh, come on!

BRIAN: It's true! His name was Mau-mau! Mau-mau the orangutang!

BILLY: You've certainly led an amazing life.

BRIAN: I sure have! I've got all kinds of stories I could tell you! Like the time I whipped three bullies all myself!

BILLY: All by yourself?

BRIAN: Yeah! And I even had a broken arm at the time!

BILLY: How did you do it?

BRIAN: With my feet! I have a black belt in karate. I learned it from an ancient Chinese master in Hong Kong. His name was Fong. Willie Fong.

BILLY: Wow! You're really something.

BRIAN: That's right. I've had more adventures than Indiana Jones. Wanna hear some more? Like the time I discovered pirate treasure in the Carribean?

BILLY: Well, maybe after Sunday school. It's about time to start.

BRIAN: Oh, yeah? What are they teaching on today?

BILLY: Lying. How wrong it is to lie about something.

BRIAN: Oh, well, I never lie. I've never lied in my life!

BILLY: Never? Not even once?

BRIAN: Not ever!

BILLY: Not even about ... trying to find the Abominable Snowman at the North Pole?

BRIAN: Well ...

BILLY: You know, lying is a terrible thing. It was the devil himself who invented the first lie. And that makes him the father of all liars.

BRIAN: He's not *my* father!

BILLY: He is when you tell a lie.

BRIAN: All right. So I exaggerated a little bit.

BILLY: Why did you do that?

BRIAN: Because ... I just wanted to be accepted and popular. My family moves around a lot and I'm never in one place very long, so it's hard to make friends.

BILLY: Brian, an exaggeration is a lie too. And pretending to be someone you're not—Jesus called that being a hypocrite.

BRIAN: You're right. I'm sorry. It's just that my real life is so dull.

BILLY: You don't have to lie to be accepted. Jesus accepts you just the way you are, and all real Christians will too. When you're a Christian, you're part of the family of God. And the family of God is everywhere, so you'll never be without friends wherever you go.

BRIAN: Really?

BILLY: Really truly. So from now on say what you mean, and mean what you say—and always tell the truth. Be a man of your word, and you'll always have plenty of friends.

BRIAN: And that's the truth!

(*Billy and Brian exit.*)

12.
The Valley Girl

(*Stacey enters.*)

STACEY: I'm bummed. Like, Suzanne was supposed to meet me here fifteen minutes ago. Then we were gonna cruise over to the bonerama and go full-sesh with Video Invaders, like really go for it. But that Suzanne just isn't with it. She is *sooo* spacey!

(*Suzanne enters out of breath.*)

SUZANNE: Sorry I'm late. Whew! I ran all the way over here. Let me catch my breath.

STACEY: Like, what's with you, Suzanne? You used to be sooooo cool. Now you're acting like a total airhead, for sure.

SUZANNE: Sorry, Stacey. I was reading my Bible and I just lost track of time.

STACEY: Reading your Bible? Like, wow, Suzanne. That's totally awesome. Like, what for? Like, don't you know that you only have to read the Bible on Sundays?

SUZANNE: I don't read the Bible because I *have* to. I *like* to read the Bible—every day.

STACEY: Like, wow, man—that's totally cosmic.

SUZANNE: I also pray every day—not just on Sundays.

STACEY: That's awesome, for sure. Like religious fanatic city.

SUZANNE: I am not a religious fanatic!

STACEY: You used to be sooooo cool, Suzanne. Like, really with it. Now you're sooooo square. Like, what happened?

SUZANNE: What happened is, I found Jesus! And I accepted Him as my Savior. Now I don't follow every fad and craze that comes along. I'm following Jesus from here on out.

STACEY: Like, far out. You're blitzing my brain, Suzanne.

SUZANNE: Would you listen to yourself? You've gone totally Val Girl.

STACEY: For sure! Like I'm really going for it to the max! It's sooooo cool. I've got the official Valley Girl handbook, the Valley Girl dictionary, and these jammin' Valley Girl clothes.

SUZANNE: I can remember when you were into preppy,

STACEY: Oh, yukko to the max! Preppy is out.

SUZANNE: And before that you were country/western—with your boots, cowboy hat, and Oak Ridge Boys albums.

STACEY: Cowboys are sooooo gruesome, like totally out of it!

SUZANNE: And before that you were even a disco queen.

STACEY: Wow, like bag my face, I'm sooooo embarrassed.

SUZANNE: See what I mean?

STACEY: You're right, Suzanne. I don't know what's cool anymore. I'm totally out of it. Like, wipe-out city!

SUZANNE: What you need is a solid foundation for your life. Something that isn't going to change with every fad ... You need Jesus. He's the same yesterday, today, and forever.

STACEY: Like, wow, Suzanne, how will I know what to do? Is there an official Jesus handbook I can follow?

SUZANNE: As a matter of fact, there is. It's called the Bible. And you need to read it every day.

STACEY: Yeah, I'm beginning to see, for sure.

SUZANNE: You also need to pray every day. When you're with your friends, you pick up the way they talk, the way they dress, and the way they act—that's how fads get started. Well, the more you're in touch with Jesus, the more like *Him* you'll become.

STACEY: But can I follow Jesus and keep my jammin' clothes?

SUZANNE: There's nothing wrong with being fashionable, or enjoying the latest fads—as long as you don't get carried away. If you put Jesus first, and examine yourself daily—to see if you're going too far with what the world is doing—then you'll have a more stable life.

STACEY: Totally awesome. I mean, like, ah, praise the Lord!

SUZANNE: Now you're getting it, Stacey. Let's go for it!

STACEY: All right! Let's go!

(*Suzanne and Stacey exit.*)

13.
Boy Fever

(*Suzanne and Stacey enter from opposite sides.*)

STACEY: Suzanne! Suzanne! Have you seen him yet?

SUZANNE: Seen who?

STACEY: Who? Who else? That new boy who's been coming to Sunday school! He's sooooo cool. He's absolutely tubular! I can hardly control myself when he's around!

SUZANNE: I must have missed him.

STACEY: Wait till he comes in! That wavy blond hair! Those blue eyes! When you see him you'll die! Absolutely die! You'll melt into your shoes!

SUZANNE: But last week you were wild about Tony.

STACEY: That was last week!

SUZANNE: And before that it was Larry.

STACEY: Larry is totally out of it! For sure. He's history!

SUZANNE: Stacey, you're something else. Are boys all you ever think about?

STACEY: Of course not! Sometimes I think about *men!* Wow! Like Tom Selleck, Tom Cruise, and Michael J. Fox—he's totally awesome to the max!

SUZANNE: But there are other things in life besides boys, you know.

STACEY: There are? Really?

SUZANNE: You know What your problem is? You've got boy fever.

STACEY: Boy fever? Oh, no! What are the symptoms?

SUZANNE: Sweaty palms, a nervous giggle, butterflies in your stomach, and a fast heartbeat whenever boys are around.

STACEY: I've got it all right. I've got boy fever.

SUZANNE: And I know just the cure.

STACEY: So do I! A boy of my very own!

SUZANNE: As a matter of fact, you're right.

STACEY: I knew you would see the light, Suzanne.

SUZANNE: And I know just the guy.

STACEY: You do?

SUZANNE: I happen to know a guy who thinks you're totally awesome to the max.

STACEY: He does? Really?

SUZANNE: That's right. And he's even written you some love letters.

STACEY: Love letters! Oh, my goodness!

SUZANNE: And what's more, he's looking for a bride!

STACEY: A b-b-b-bride?

SUZANNE: Not right away—but down the road a little.

STACEY: He sounds perfect! Who is it? Don't keep me in suspense! Does he go to church here?

SUZANNE: Yes—in a manner of speaking.

STACEY: Then who is it?

SUZANNE: His name is ... Jesus.

STACEY: Jesus! Oh, Suzanne! I thought you were serious!

SUZANNE: I am! He loves you more than anyone! And His love letters to you are in the Bible!

STACEY: You know what my problem is? The boys I like never seem to like me.

SUZANNE: That's called unrequited love—when you love some one who doesn't love you back. And that's Jesus' biggest heartbreak. He loves the world so much—and most of the world ignores Him.

STACEY: Well, I don't ignore Him.

SUZANNE: But you need to fall in love with Him. Fall in love with Jesus first, and then your relationships with boys will always be in their proper place. In other words, you won't go "boy crazy." And your boy fever will always be kept under control.

STACEY: Right you are, Suzanne. From now on I'm turning over a new leaf. No more hanging around boys all the time. From now on—no more boy fever!

SUZANNE: Now you're talking, Stacey.

STACEY: Oh, no! Look! Over there! He just came in the door! The new boy! Blond hair! Blue eyes! Oh, Suzanne! I'm melting I'm melting, I'm mmmeeellltttiiinnnggg ...

(*Stacey drops out of sight.*)

SUZANNE: Worst case of boy fever I've ever seen!

(*Suzanne exits.*)

14.
Junk Food

(*Suzanne and Stacey enter from opposite directions.*)

SUZANNE: Hi, Stacey. Are you ready for the party tonight?

STACEY: For sure. To the max. I've even got all the snack foods ready. Like, we're gonna have some kind of party!

SUZANNE: Sounds great. What did you get?

STACEY: Like, nothing but the best for *my* friends. I've got Cheese Chewies, Choco Cakes, Winkies, Pinkies, and Blinkies, Chewy Chunkos, Woa Woas, Gooboos, Jelly Wellies, and Gummy Yummies. All my favorites. We're going to pig-out and grub down, for sure.

SUZANNE: Oh, Stacey, all that is junk food! Do you really eat that stuff?

STACEY: Sure. Like, all the time.

SUZANNE: Stacey to borrow a phrase from you, yukko to the max!

STACEY: What's wrong?

SUZANNE: All those things aren't good for you. They're so artificial!

STACEY: Artificial?

SUZANNE: When's the last time you saw a Gummy Yummy growing from a tree?

STACEY: But they're just harmless little snackie-wackies.

SUZANNE: Those harmless little snackie-wackies are loaded with sugar, artificial coloring, artificial flavorings, and preservatives. Didn't you ever learn about nutrition and proper eating in school?

STACEY: It was not my best subject. Like, I even used to sneak chocolate bars during health class.

SUZANNE: Stacey!

STACEY: I know. What a bummer, for sure. So now how am I supposed to know what's good for me?

SUZANNE: It's not that difficult to know what's

good for us. The Lord designed our bodies, and at the same time made us lots of good, natural food to eat. Lots of different and delicious fresh fruits and vegetables. And you can be sure that the farther we get from natural foods, the sooner we'll get into trouble.

STACEY: But, Suzanne, you don't understand. I've *got* to have my Jelly Wellies!

SUZANNE: If you keep eating Jelly Wellies, you'll soon have a jelly belly.

STACEY: Oh, I never worry about calories. I eat a light lunch.

SUZANNE: Like what?

STACEY: Usually a diet soft drink and potato chips.

SUZANNE: Stacey! You're a regular junk food junkie!

STACEY: Wow, like bag my face with a sack of chocolate chip cookies! I'm so embarrassed.

SUZANNE: The Lord wants us to be healthy. But we have to cooperate. If we constantly do things that are bad for us, can we really blame the Lord if we get sick?

STACEY: Maybe that's why I've been feeling so run down lately,

SUZANNE: That could be, Stacey. You definitely need to change your diet to healthier foods. What do you usually have for breakfast?

STACEY: Usually I skip breakfast. But sometimes I have a chocolate donut and coffee.

SUZANNE: That's not very good fuel for your body, Stacey. How about good whole wheat bread, fresh fruit, and an egg instead? That will get your day off to a good start. You've got to start taking better care of yourself.

STACEY: For sure.

SUZANNE: And you need to have a better lunch. A sandwich, more fruit, and maybe some soup. What do you usually have for supper?

STACEY: I always have a good supper. My mother sees to that.

SUZANNE: Good for her!

STACEY: What else can I do?

SUZANNE: How about remembering those people around the world who don't have enough to eat, let alone a lot of junk food. For the most part, we're very blessed in America. But let's not forget the poor.

STACEY: But what can I do to help the poor?

SUZANNE: How about taking some of the money you spend on Jelly Wellies and other junk foods and giving it to some charity or missionary organization?

STACEY: That's a good idea. For sure. But, what about tonight's party?

SUZANNE: I'll help you make some *real* snack foods out of some *real* food.

STACEY: Like, you are totally awesome, Suzanne. Like, a real friend.

SUZANNE: Anytime, Stacey. And the next time you get the urge to eat a Chewy Chunko, just ask yourself—why do they call it "junk" food?

STACEY: Because it belongs in the trash can—but not in my stomach!

SUZANNE: Right on, Stacey! Let's go get some real food!

STACEY: I'm with you! Let's go!

(*Suzanne and Stacey exit.*)

15.
Idols

(*Stacey enters.*)

STACEY: Wow, let's see if I've got everything … I've got my Michael Jackson T-shirt, my Michael Jackson poster, my Michael Jackson photographs, my Michael Jackson button, my Michael Jackson Records, my official authentic, limited-edition Michael Jackson jeweled glove, my Michael Jackson books and magazines, and my Michael Jackson limited-edition dark glasses.

(*Suzanne enters.*)

SUZANNE: Hi, Stacey. Whatcha doing?

STACEY: Like, wow Suzanne, I'm taking inventory of my Michael Jackson souvenirs. Do you know anything else I can buy to remind me of Michael Jackson? He's the greatest, he's a dream, and he's sooooo cute, for sure. Like awesome to the max!

SUZANNE: I think you've got everything that can be bought. Don't you think you've gone a bit overboard?

STACEY: But he's such a doll! That's it! A Michael Jackson doll! Surely there's a Michael Jackson doll I can buy!

SUZANNE: I don't know about you, Stacey.

STACEY: What do you mean, Suzanne?

SUZANNE: I can remember when you were wild over Barry Manilow.

STACEY: Oh, Suzanne, he's totally out of it. Like a real has-been, for sure.

SUZANNE: And before that it was the Bee Gees.

STACEY: Oh, wow, like bag my face. Don't tell anybody that, Suzanne, I'm sooooo embarrassed.

SUZANNE: And a year from now it will be somebody else. There's nothing wrong with admiring somebody, or having a hero, but you shouldn't get so carried away. Famous people come and go. Only Jesus is here to stay.

STACEY: But surely listening to some fast music won't do any harm.

SUZANNE: It depends on what the songs are saying. Whenever you listen to music, it's like planting a seed in your head. If you're not careful, some very bad thoughts can take root and grow. Now, Stacey, you've got to admit it, in a lot of modern songs, Christian values are thrown out the door. And a lot of flash and glitter are used to sell the world's values.

STACEY: I don't know, Suzanne.

SUZANNE: Stacey . . . if you eat junk food, watch junk television, read junk magazines, listen to junk music, speak junk words, think junk thoughts, and see junk movies . . . What does that make you?

STACEY: Wow, like a regular junk pile.

SUZANNE: Exactly!

STACEY: Come on, Suzanne, don't you like listening to some wild music sometimes?

SUZANNE: I can't. I don't have any ears.

STACEY: What?! Then what are those things on each side of your head?

SUZANNE: You mean these ears?

STACEY: Yeah!

SUZANNE: I gave those ears to Jesus long ago.

STACEY: But whenever you hear fast music, doesn't it make you want to pick up your feet and dance?

SUZANNE: I can't. I don't have any feet.

STACEY: Then what are those things at the bottom of your legs?

SUZANNE: I gave those feet to Jesus a long time ago. In fact, I've given my whole body to Jesus.

STACEY: Far out, Suzanne, you're blowing my mind—for sure.

SUZANNE: If you're going to get wrapped up in somebody, get wrapped up in Jesus. He never changes. He's the greatest. Everyone else shrinks to insignificance in comparison with Him. And He loves you, watches over you, and cares for you. Many rock stars are only in it for what they can get. Jesus, the rock of our salvation, is in it for what He can give.

STACEY: I'm beginning to see your point, Suzanne, for sure. So let's make like you-know-who and "beat it" to someplace else where I can get away from all this stuff.

SUZANNE: I'm with you, Stacey. Let's go.

(*Suzanne and Stacey exit.*)

16. The Whiner

(*A man and woman enter.*)

WOMAN: What a beautiful day to have a picnic.

MAN (*speaking in a whiny voice*): But why do we have to eat at *this* picnic table?

WOMAN: What's wrong with it?

MAN: I don't like it.

WOMAN: Why?

MAN: It's too old.

WOMAN: What difference does it make? Besides, it's such a nice spot.

MAN: What's so nice about it?

WOMAN: Well, we're right by that tree for one thing.

MAN: I don't like that tree.

WOMAN: Why not?

MAN: It's not tall enough. There's not enough shade. And it doesn't even have a squirrel in it. I want a tree that has a squirrel in it.

WOMAN: We're staying right here!

MAN: But the other side of the park is better.

WOMAN: It is not.

MAN: It is so. And we're too far from the playground over here.

WOMAN: We are not.

MAN: We are to!

WOMAN: Just enjoy the beautiful weather.

MAN: I can't.

WOMAN: Why not?

MAN: It's too hot.

WOMAN: It is not!

MAN: It is too! And it's too humid! And there's not enough of a breeze blowing!

WOMAN: Would you stop being so picky?

MAN: I am not being picky! And you know what else? There's too many bugs over here. On the other side of the park there aren't this many bugs.

WOMAN: Don't be ridiculous! Bugs don't fly over here more than they do over there!

MAN: They do so.

WOMAN: How do you know?

MAN: I just know, that's how I know!

WOMAN: I give up! Just pick up the picnic basket and we'll move to the other side of the park.

MAN: But the picnic basket's too heavy!

WOMAN: It is not! It's only got some chicken inside!

MAN: Chicken! I don't like cold chicken!

WOMAN: Then we'll barbecue it on the park's grill.

MAN: But the grill's too dirty.

WOMAN: So we'll clean the grill!

MAN: But that's too much work! We're supposed to relax on a picnic!

WOMAN: Would you stop whining about everything? I've had it up to here with your complaining! Can't you be thankful about something for a change?

MAN: There's nothing to be thankful for!

WOMAN: The Bible says, "in everything give thanks, for this is the will of God." If you'd stop whining long enough to count your blessings, you'd enjoy life a little bit more.

MAN: Blessings? What blessings?

WOMAN: You're healthy aren't you?

MAN: Well . . . yes.

WOMAN: And you live in the United States of America—that's a pretty great blessing.

MAN: I guess you're right. But what about people who don't have all those blessings?

WOMAN: If people who are in need and in trouble would turn to the Lord, He could change their lives and meet their needs. They can be thankful right now that there is always hope in the Lord, and that the door to His bountiful supply is always open.

MAN: I guess knowing the Lord is the greatest blessing of all, isn't it?

WOMAN: That's right.

MAN: You know, that is a pretty nice tree. And the grass under my feet is suddenly looking just as green as the grass on the other side of the park.

WOMAN: Now you're talking.

MAN: Everything looks brighter and better when you have a thankful attitude. I think I could even eat cold chicken!

WOMAN: It's a miracle! When we get home, I'll fix my spinach souffle!

MAN: Now let's not get carried away! Nobody could be thankful for your spinach souffle!

WOMAN: I guess I pushed you a little too far. All right, no more spinach souffle.

MAN: Well, praise the Lord! Now *that* I can be thankful for!

(*The man and woman exit.*)

17.
Parts Is Parts

(*The cashier and man enter from opposite sides.*)

CASHIER: Hello sir, and welcome to Fast Food Delight. May I take your order?

MAN: I don't know. What you got?

CASHIER: We've got everything! Burgers—both fried and charcoal broiled, tacos, fish, hot dogs, pizza, and golden fried chicken made from 100 percent real parts of chicken.

MAN: I don't know. I'm not really very hungry.

CASHIER: Why is that?

MAN: Oh, I'm just depressed. Really depressed.

CASHIER: Well, for what reason?

MAN: I don't know. It just seems like in my whole life everything has gone wrong. Nothing ever works out right for me.

CASHIER: In that case I know just what you need.

MAN: What's that? The chicken parts?

CASHIER: Nope. What you need is Jesus.

MAN: Jesus?

CASHIER: That's right. See, your problem is that you have a broken life. Your dreams have been broken apart, your hopes shattered, everything crushed.

MAN: That's right. Exactly right. But where does Jesus fit in?

CASHIER: Well, as I hear tell, God takes all the respective parts of a broken life and puts them back together.

MAN: What parts?

CASHIER: Every part! Parts is parts! And He *fuses* them back together.

MAN: Then what?

CASHIER: Then He burns all the imperfections out of our life.

MAN: B-b-burns?

CASHIER: That's right.

MAN: What happens next?

CASHIER: Then He molds and shapes every-thing back together even better than it was before!

MAN: B-b-better?

CASHIER: That's right. And He can make a life that was a failure into a success. You know what happens then?

MAN: What?

CASHIER: Then God can spice up your life with all kinds of special ingredients! He can lay you down on a bed of peace, cover you with the sauce of the Holy Spirit, put you between the bread of life, quench your thirst with the milk of the Word, and then feed you with the meat of Christian living!

MAN: Sounds mighty good!

CASHIER: That's what you call ordering life with everything! And God even has carry-outs! One of these days He's going to carry us out of this world!

MAN: You know, I think I'll take Jesus. And I feel better already.

CASHIER: Then perhaps you'd also like to try our golden fried chicken, made from 100 percent real parts of chicken.

MAN: I don't think so. Suddenly, I have a craving for Wendy's food.

CASHIER: But why? Foods is foods, meats is meats, and parts is parts.

MAN: But some parts is better than other parts.

CASHIER: That's true. Well, have a nice day any-way.... (*The man exits and a lady enters.*) Hello ma'am, and welcome to Fast Food De-light. May I help you?

LADY: Where's the beef?!!!

CASHIER: Well, as I hear tell, God owns the cat-tle on a thousand hills—that's what it says in the Bible—so I reckon *He's* got the beef!

LADY: Ohhhhhh....

(*The cashier and the lady exit.*)

18.
Methuselah

(*The reporter and Methuselah enter.*)

REPORTER: Hello and welcome to this special report brought to you by the Genesis Bible Book of World Records. The book that tells you the biggest, the smallest, the highest, the lowest, the hottest, the coldest, the richest, the poorest, the fastest, the slowest, and so on and so forth. Today we are going to meet an individual whose unique accomplishment has entitled him to a place in the Genesis Book of World Records. He is the world's *oldest* man. May we have your name sir?

METH: Methuselah.

REPORTER: And just how old are you?

METH: This year I'll be 969 years *young*.

REPORTER: That's amazing! To what do you owe your longevity?

METH: Well, several things. I never eat fried foods, I work out at Gold's Gym several times a week, I keep out of small foreign cars, and when I do drive, I always fasten my seat belt. But I guess the major thing that has kept me going all these years is that I love the Lord with all my heart and I listen to Him when He tells me how to live.

REPORTER: You lead a very active life. Did yor ever consider retiring?

METH: Yeah, I considered it when I was 478—that's when most of my friends retired. So I quit my job and went down to Florida for a while—about a hundred years. But I got bored.

REPORTER: So what are you doing now?

METH: These are exciting times to be alive! It doesn't matter what your age is! There are so many things to do in the kingdom of God! The Lord is coming back to this earth soon, and He's busy working through His children to reach out to this world one last time.

REPORTER: In 900 years I'll bet you've seen a lot of changes in this world.

METH: Yes—most of them bad.

REPORTER: Really? What are some of the bad changes you've seen?

METH: For one thing, the younger generation has no respect for their elders.

REPORTER: What do you mean by the "younger generation"?

METH: Anyone under 900 years old.

REPORTER: I see.

METH: You know, some of us older folks have been around for quite a while, and we've learned a few things—if only younger people would listen!

REPORTER: Do you realize that being the world's oldest man entitles you to a place in the Genesis Book of World Records?

METH: So what? I'd rather have a place in the Lamb's Book of Life.

REPORTER: What's that?

METH: Well, the lamb—that's Jesus Christ. He was the lamb that God offered as a sacrifice for the sins of the whole world. And He keeps a book in Heaven. And in the book is written the names of all the people who accept Jesus as their Lord and Savior.

REPORTER: Do you have any parting words you'd like to give us? Perhaps something you've learned in your long life?

METH: Yes. Listen, children, this is 969 years talking to you. You want to live a long and happy life? Just keep a smile on your face, a spring in your step, and the Lord Jesus Christ in your heart. And keep busy for Jesus. There's still a lot to be done before He comes back. And if you'll do that, the world may fall around you, but you'll be all right—safe in the arms of God.

REPORTER: Thank you, Methuselah.

METH: You're welcome. Now you'll have to excuse me. I'm late for my aerobics class.

REPORTER: An oldtimer like you goes to an aerobics class?

METH: I *teach* the aerobics class! Who do you think taught Jane Fonda everything she knows? One and two and stretch and pull! All right! Let's go!

(*The reporter and Methuselah exit.*)

19. Where's the Belief?

(*The cashier and a lady enters from opposite directions.*)

CASHIER: Hello ma'am, and welcome to Fast Food Delight. May I help you?

LADY: Where's the belief?!

CASHIER: I beg your pardon?

LADY: Where's the belief?!

CASHIER: I'm afraid I don't understand.

LADY: I don't either, that's the problem!

CASHIER: I see. Perhaps you could explain further.

LADY: Sometimes when I pray, I don't get any answers! Sometimes ... I don't think there's anybody up there. I really don't.

CASHIER: You know, sometimes God has to have time to assemble all the respective parts of the answer to your prayer before He can give it to you.

LADY: He does?

CASHIER: That's right. You see that painting on the wall?

LADY: You mean of that man over there?

CASHIER: Yes, ma'am. That's our founder, Colonel Alfred D. Gizzard. He does fast food right!

LADY: He's kinda cute.

CASHIER: Well, Colonel Gizzard's motto was, "We will sell no gizzards before their time." The trouble with life today is everything is instant and fast. Fast food, fast cars, fast exercise, fast work, fast prayers. And we expect God to be just as fast. We don't have the patience to allow Him to work in His own time.

LADY: Ohhhhh . . .

CASHIER: You know, we serve a nice God.

LADY: A nice, *big* God.

CASHIER: A nice, big, *loving* God.

LADY: A nice, big, loving, *prayer-answering* God.

CASHIER: A nice, big, loving, prayer-answering, *miracle-working* God.

LADY: So where's the belief?

CASHIER: Well, some people have belief—that is, faith—and some people don't.

LADY: So how do I get some? I'm tired of fluffy religious buns! I want some beef! And beef is belief in God!

CASHIER: Well, it says in the Bible that faith comes from hearing and reading the Word of God. You need to fill yourself with scriptures, and then the Holy Spirit can start building faith in your life.

LADY: That sounds good to me, Sonny.

CASHIER: You know, it's hard to have faith when you fill your mind and heart with worldly things, read worldly magazines and books, speak worldly words, and watch Godless television shows.

LADY: You've got a point there.

CASHIER: You could say that building faith is like cooking chili—you need to add the right ingredients, stir it up occasionally, and practice making it often.

LADY: I see what you mean.

CASHIER: All of us have some faith—Jesus brings it with Him when He enters our heart. So you could say that we need to have faith in our own faith.

LADY: Say what? Faith in our own faith?

CASHIER: That's right. Believe in God, and believe in yourself. As long as you think you don't have enough faith, you'll never use what you've got. Muscle grows when you exercise it, and so does faith.

LADY: I'll tell that to my aerobics class!

CASHIER: And another thing, whenever you pray, make sure your prayers are specific. If someone were to drive by our drive-thru window and say, "I want food!"—that would be a hard order to fill. So be specific. And speaking of food, perhaps you'd like to order our famous golden fried chicken made from 100 percent real parts of chicken.

LADY: Are you kidding? The advice here is great—but your food is terrible.

CASHIER: That's true. Well, have a nice day anyway.

LADY: Give my regards to Colonel Gizzard! He's a real cutie! Ha! Ha! Ha!

(*The cashier and lady exit.*)

20.
King Solomon

(*The reporter and King Solomon enters.*)

REPORTER: Ladies and gentlemen! On this incredible edition of the Genesis Book of World Records, we bring you a world record holder in not one, but several categories. May we have your name, sir?

KING: Solomon.

REPORTER: And what's so special about you?

KING: I'm the wisest man in the world.

REPORTER: Really? Wow! Did you ever consider appearing on some game shows? You could make a fortune!

KING: I don't need to. I'm also the richest man in the world.

REPORTER: I see.

KING: I'm also the greatest king in the world with the greatest kingdom in the world.

REPORTER: And you're also the humblest man in the world right?

KING: It's hard to be humble when you're as great as I am. I mean, we're not talking minor greatness here, we're talking *major* greatness.

REPORTER: And how did you become all those things?

KING: It all comes through being wise. That's the key.

REPORTER: You must have spent many years in college to become so smart.

KING: Nope. That's not how I became wise.

REPORTER: Then you must be self-taught. You must have read a lot books.

KING: Going to school and reading are important, but in my case my intelligence and understanding came directly from the Lord. I asked him for wisdom to rule my people, and He gave it to me.

REPORTER: So you're a special case.

KING: Not really. Anybody can have this wisdom from God. All they have to do is ask Him for it, and study God's Word—the greatest guidebook in the world!

REPORTER: But what about all the people in the world who are educated, but who don't know God? Are they wise?

KING: The reverence and respect for God is the beginning of all wisdom. In other words, if you don't know Jesus, you don't know anything yet! Because it's not always *what* you know, it's *who* you know.

REPORTER: But if you *do* know Jesus. . . .

KING: Then you have a special advantage over those who don't.

REPORTER: Since you're the wisest man in the world, let me ask you some questions I'm sure a lot of people have wondered about. For instance, what's the best way to become rich? Stocks and bonds maybe?

KING: The blessing of the Lord, it maketh rich, and He adds no sorrow with it.

REPORTER: What's the best way to deal with your enemies?

KING: When a man's ways please the Lord, He makes even his enemies to be at peace with him.

REPORTER: What's the best thing to do when trouble comes your way?

KING: The name of the Lord is a strong tower; the righteous man runs into it, and is safe.

REPORTER: What about this physical fitness craze? Is that a good thing?

KING: The glory of a young man is his strength. . . .

REPORTER: But what about women?

KING: A virtuous woman surrounds herself with strength, and makes her arms strong.

REPORTER: What's the best way to make decisions?

KING: Trust in the Lord with all your heart, and lean not on your own understanding. In all your ways acknowledge Him, and He will direct your paths.

REPORTER: Remarkable!

KING: All of these truths and a whole lot more are in the Bible in the book of Proverbs, which the Holy Spirit moved me to write. And now I've got a question for you.

REPORTER: For *me*?

KING: Yes. What famous celebrity first uttered these words: "Watch out, big boys!"

REPORTER: That's easy! It was Mary Lou Retton.

KING: Wrong! It was my father, King David, who first said that.

REPORTER: When did he say that?

KING: When he first saw the Philistines! He said, "Watch out, big boys! Here I come in the name of the Lord!"

REPORTER: Well, well, you learn something new every day.

KING: You do if you want to be wise.

REPORTER: So there you have it, ladies and gentlemen, this is the Genesis Book of World Records signing off!

(*The reporter and King Solomon exit.*)

22.
Real Puppets

ANNOUNCER: It's now time for ... Real Puppets! The show that brings you puppets from all walks of life. Some walk, some talk, some fight, and some even bite. And now here's your host.

(The host and Eve enter.)

HOST: Hello and welcome to ... Real Puppets. Today we have a very special guest. Straight from the pages of the Bible, *and* the Genesis Book of World Records, we have with us the world's very first woman! So let's give a *real* warm *Real* Puppets welcome to—Eve.

EVE: Hello. It's a *real* pleasure to be here.

HOST: Eve, there's something I've always wondered. Do you have a last name?

EVE: No. It's just "Eve." Back in the old days, there was no need for last names. There were so few of us that there were plenty of names to go around. There was only one Adam, one Eve, one Cain, one Abel, one George ...

HOST: I see.

EVE: One Methuselah, one Sidney, one Gonzales ...

HOST: We get the idea.

EVE: One Antionio, one Lucy, one Sylvester ...

HOST: All right, already!

EVE: And for a long time we didn't even need zip codes. There was only one address–the Garden of Eden.

HOST: I'm sure all of us are curious about what life was like in the Garden of Eden.

EVE: It was wonderful! All the animals were tame. We all got along with one another. There was very little work to do, and plenty of time to enjoy life.

HOST: Sounds like a *real* paradise.

EVE: Better than Fantasy Island!

HOST: What did you eat in the garden?

EVE: Mostly fast foods.

HOST: You mean like McDonald's?

EVE: No! No! A lot faster than McDonald's! Whenever we'd get hungry, we'd just go pick some fruit off the trees or vegetables out of the ground

HOST: Speaking of food, is it true that you ate of the forbidden fruit?

EVE: Yeah ... I gave into temptation–and we lost everything!

HOST: But didn't you know better?

EVE: Sure. We didn't have the Bible in those days, but we talked to God face-to-face. We knew what was right and what was wrong.

HOST: Then why did you give in?

EVE: Because I listened to the devil instead of the Lord. The devil entered into a serpent and lied to me! Tricked me! That no-good, good-for-nothing, low-down, vicious, vile, evil, corrupt, rotten, fiendish, dirty, degenerate, sneaky, slimy, scaly, overgrown worm!

HOST: You can say that again!

EVE: That no-good, good-for-nothing, low-down . . .

HOST: No! Wait! We don't have the time. Just tell us what happened next.

EVE: Well, I didn't give into temptation right away. My first mistake was listening to the devil. Then I started desiring the forbidden fruit myself—in spite of the Lord's warning not to eat it. So I just kind of strolled over to the forbidden fruit and looked at it awhile.

HOST: But you didn't eat it?

EVE: Not right away. After I'd looked it over, I leaned over and smelled it. It sure smelled good. Then I touched it and felt it awhile. And then I *picked it!* And you know what happened?

HOST: What?

EVE: Nothing. No lightening out of the sky, no loud voice from God. So then I figured, I've come this far and nothing bad has happened—I might as well go all the way! So I ate it!

HOST: When did you realize that you had sinned?

EVE: Right then and there! My eyes were suddenly opened to what I had done, and I felt terrible!

HOST: Then why did you go ahead and give some of the fruit to Adam?

EVE: I hate to say it, but when you give into temptation and sin, you feel better if others are doing it with you. So you draw them into it, or you join others who are already doing the same thing. So that makes it a double sin.

HOST: What did you learn from your experience?

EVE: After our sin, our lives were ruined! We had to work for a living. No more paradise! So listen, don't give into temptation! Read the Bible and pray so you know what's right and what's wrong. Don't listen to the devil, or the world, or your friends, or anyone else who tries to tempt you! Learn from *my* mistake. *Don't give in to sin!*

HOST: Thank you, Eve, for being our guest. And that's all for today for Real Puppets! So long!

(*The host and Eve exit.*)

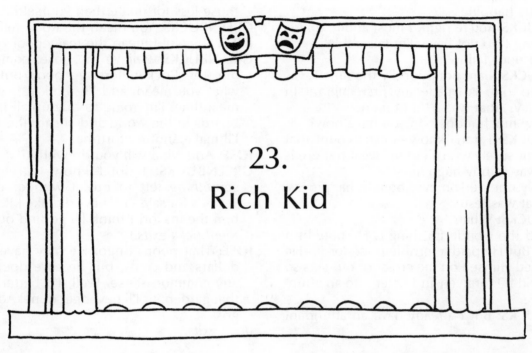

23.
Rich Kid

(*Greenbucks enters.*)

GREENBUCKS: I'm bored. Here I have all the money in the world, but I don't know what to do with it. I already own everything. I even have my own butler . . . Smedley! Come here a minute!

(*Smedley enters.*)

SMEDLEY: Yes, Master Greenbucks?

GREENBUCKS: I want you to go buy Disney World—I'm gonna turn it into my own private playground.

SMEDLEY: Yes, Master Greenbucks. Whatever you say, sir. And by the way, the new gardener is here to see you.

GREENBUCKS: Send him in.

SMEDLEY: Yes, sir.

(*Smedley exits. José enters.*)

JOSÉ: Hola! Hola! (pronounced, "ola.") . . . Buenas noches! You the head honcho around here?

GREENBUCKS: I am Reginald Oliver Greenbucks the Third!

JOSÉ: Happy to meet you. I am José Felipe Eduardo Lopez Alejandro Devega Maximillian Hernandez Ricardo Miguel Vincenti Ortega Diego Juarez DeAngelo Reynosa the First! But you can call me José. I have seven brothers and two sisters—but don't ask me their names or we'll be here all day.

GREENBUCKS: I understand that you're the best gardener in the world.

JOSÉ: I don't know about that, senor.

GREENBUCKS: Well, you'd better be. I have a garden the size of Detroit.

JOSÉ: Aay yi yi!

GREENBUCKS: Everything I have is the biggest and the best. I even have the biggest dog in the world.

JOSÉ: You do?

GREENBUCKS: Sure! I'll show you! Here boy! Here boy! Over here!

(*A huge dog enters.*)

DOG: Arf! Arf!

JOSÉ: Ayyyy! That *is* a big dog!

GREENBUCKS: I call him . . . Howard Humongus.

DOG: Arf! Arf!

GREENBUCKS: Down, Howard, down boy! Go play with that gold bone I bought you.

(*Dog exits, barking.*)

JOSÉ: You must be pretty rich.

GREENBUCKS: I'm the richest guy in the world! Whatever I want, I buy.

JOSÉ: I know something you can't buy.

GREENBUCKS: Nonsense! I can afford anything!

JOSÉ: You can buy enchiladas, burritos, tacos, tostadas, tamales, and nachos ... But you can't buy happiness.

GREENBUCKS: You're right. I must admit, that is one thing I do not have. I'm miserable.

JOSÉ: You poor fellow.

GREENBUCKS: I am not poor! By the time I was six years old, I'd made my first million! In those days, that was a lot of money.

JOSÉ: How much money do you have now?

GREENBUCKS: I don't know—I can't count that high. But surely with all of my wealth there is some way to buy happiness!

JOSÉ: Only one person ever bought happiness. And that was Jesus.

GREENBUCKS: What?

JOSÉ: And the wonderful thing is He bought it for us. But He paid a terrible price for it—He sacrificed Himself on the cross for our sins so we could be forgiven and enter into an abundant life.

GREENBUCKS: But I already have an abundant life.

JOSÉ: An abundant life doesn't necessarily mean riches. It can mean peace, joy, happiness, love ... All the things money can't buy, but things that enrich our lives.

GREENBUCKS: How can I get those things?

JOSÉ: Accept Jesus as your Savior and put *Him* first in your life—not your money, or money-making ability. Keep His commandments and don't hold anything back, and *then* you'll be happy! Why don't you start off by helping those less fortunate than yourself?

GREENBUCKS: You mean the Rockefellers?

JOSÉ: No, No! I mean the *really* poor people.

GREENBUCKS: Believe me, José, compared to me, the Rockefellers *are* poor. But I know what you mean, and I'll think it over. In the meantime, I'm going to buy up all the skateboards in the world and corner the market— I'll make another fortune.

JOSÉ: And what will you do with it?

GREENBUCKS: I don't know—surely there's *something* left to buy. I wonder if Dallas, Texas is for sale—I always did like J.R. I'll make him the mayor! I think I'll go find out.

(*Greenbucks exits.*)

JOSÉ: That poor gringo. He may have a lot of dollars and cents, but he sure doesn't have any common sense. Well, I'd better start on that garden, or I'll never get done! Adios, amigos!

(*José exits.*)

24. The Second Honeymooners

(*Allyse and Alf enter from opposite directions.*)
ALF: All right, Allyse, where is it?
ALLYSE: Where's what, Alf?
ALF: What else? My bowling ball! You're always hiding my bowling ball!
ALLYSE: A bowling ball is kind of big to hide, Alf! It's not exactly something you'd put in your pocket!

ALF: I'm serious, Allyse …
ALLYSE: Oh, Alf, here we are on a once-in-a-life-time cruise in the Carribean—and all you can think of is bowling! You never would have come if I hadn't found a ship with a bowling alley!
ALF: Well, what else is there to do on this ship?
ALLYSE: Lay in the sun and relax.

ALF: I'd look like a beached whale in a bathing suit! Come on, Allyse, where is it?!

ALLYSE: For the last time, I don't know where your stupid bowling ball is! For all I know, it could have rolled off the ship into the ocean! And I hope it did!

(*Allyse exits.*)

ALF: One of these days, Allyse, you're really going places! You know where you're going? To the moon!

(*Horton enters.*)

HORTON: Hey, Alfie boy!

ALF: There you are! Where you been all this time, Horton? I haven't seen you since this cruise started.

HORTON: I been way down in the lowest part of the ship.

ALF: That figures.

HORTON: Boy, you should see the pipes on this ship! Say, maybe you could help me figure out something.

ALF: What?

HORTON: When you flush a toilet on one of these ships—where does the waste go? I mean, a ship doesn't have sewers, you know what I mean? I lay awake at night thinking about that.

ALF: Who cares, Horton?

HORTON: Hey, what's the matter, Alfie boy?

ALF: Just leave me alone.

HORTON: But you're so uptight! You gotta loosen up! Like those aerobics instructors. (He demonstrates.) Hip Hip hi hi heh heh!

ALF: Now cut that out! Listen, have you seen my bowling ball?

HORTON: Was it big, round, and black with holes in it?

ALF: Yeah! That's it!

HORTON: No—I haven't seen it.

ALF: Aw! Horton!

HORTON: Hey, Alfie, where's Allyse?

ALF: I don't know. We just had a fight.

HORTON: Not again!

ALF: Yeah. I don't know what's wrong with me, Horton.

HORTON: You gotta learn to be nice, be gentle, be kind—like it says in the Bible. That's some of those fruits of the Spirit. You gotta learn to get along better with your fellow man—and woman.

ALF: Oh, Horton, it's too late for me. I'm hopeless.

HORTON: Hey, nobody's hopeless when they've got Jesus on their side. He can give you the right spirit if you allow him some room in your heart.

ALF: Really, Horton? He could change even me?

HORTON: He can change anybody!

ALF: But I'm just a big bag of hot air.

HORTON: So? He can let some of that hot air out.

ALF: But it's too late—Allyse will never forgive me.

(*Allyse enters.*)

ALLYSE: Your wrong, Alf.

ALF: Allyse!

ALLYSE: I've heard what you just said. And if you're willing to try and change with God's help, I'll give you another chance. Just like Jesus needs to make you more gentle, He needs to make me more forgiving.

ALF: Allyse, you're the greatest!

HORTON: (*Crying*) Aw, Alf, That's beautiful ...

ALF: Come on, Allyse, let's go play some shuffleboard or something. Let's start enjoying this cruise.

ALLYSE: I'm with you, Alf.

ALF: Come on, Horton, you can come too.

HORTON: All right, Alfie! I'm with you! Let's go shuffle those boards—whatever that is!

(*They all exit.*)

25.
Secret Agent

(*Alpha enters.*)

ALPHA: Good, nobody's around. Now's my chance to call headquarters and find out my next secret mission. I'll raise the antenna on my secret shoe radio.... (*an antenna rises up*) there.... Now to place the call. This is secret agent Double-O-Alpha calling headquarters. Come in, chief!

VOICE: This is secret headquarters. What are the passwords?

ALPHA: E.T. phone home. I repeat, E.T. phone home

VOICE: Very good, Double-O-Alpha.

ALPHA: What's my next assignment, chief?

VOICE: Double-O-Alpha, this will be the most important assignment of your life. The fate of the entire world hangs in the balance. This is the big one, Double-O-Alpha.

ALPHA: I'm ready when you are, chief. Lay it on me.

VOICE: This is too important for radio transmission. I must make sure you understand perfectly what you're supposed to do.

ALPHA: So how do I get my instructions?

VOICE: You are to meet secret agent Double-O-Omega on the corner of Secret Street and

Confidential Boulevard. He well give you your next assignment.

ALPHA: Got you, chief! I'm on my way!

VOICE: This is headquarters signing off.

ALPHA: Over and out!

(*The antenna goes down and he exits. He enters again a few seconds later.*)

ALPHA: Well, here I am on the corner of Secret Street and Confidential Boulevard. But where's my contact? (*A man enters.*) Aha! There's a secret agent if I ever saw one. I'll try the password on him.... (*Clears throat.*) Excuse me....

MAN: Yeah?

ALPHA: Fuzzy Wuzzy was a bear.

MAN: What? What are you? Some kind of nut? A guy can't even walk down the street anymore without running into a crazy person!

(*The man exits. Omega enters behind Alpha.*)

OMEGA (*wearing glasses and fake nose*): Excuse me, did I hear you say something about a bear?

ALPHA: I said, Fuzzy Wuzzy was a bear ...

OMEGA: Fuzzy Wuzzy had no hair ...

ALPHA: Fuzzy Wuzzy wasn't fuzzy was he? ... You're secret agent Double-O-Omega!

OMEGA: Right. And you're Double-O-Alpha.

ALPHA: That's a great disguise!

OMEGA: Thank you. Are you ready to receive your assignment?

ALPHA: Yes! What is it?

OMEGA: First, I have to give you the secret message; listen very closely. "Everyone has sinned and cut themselves off from God, but Jesus was sent by God to seek and to save the lost, and bring people back into a right relationship with God. Everyone who confesses his sins, and receives Jesus as his Savior, has a brand new life here on earth, and will live forever with God,"—got that?

ALPHA: Got it! I'll guard this secret message with my life. No one will ever know!

OMEGA: Wait a minute! Your assignment is to tell *everyone* this message!

ALPHA: What? But I can't be a secret agent if I go around telling everybody secret messages!

OMEGA: There are no *secret* Christians! Are you a follower of Jesus?

ALPHA: Yes.

OMEGA: Well, that means you're a disciple. And if you're a disciple, that means you have to teach and preach and spread this message—the gospel. That's your assignment—tell the message to the world. That's every Christian's assignment—so you won't be working alone.

ALPHA: But how will I do it?

OMEGA: Any way you can! Tell them personally, through books, tracts, television, movies, posters, bumper stickers, cards, letters—shout it from the housetops! I understand some people even spread this message through puppet shows!

ALPHA: I'll do it!

OMEGA: Good. Remember, the fate of the world hangs in the balance. Good luck, Double-O-Alpha.

(*Omega exits.*)

ALPHA: Well, if I'm going to spread the gospel, I might as well start right here. Let's see ... I know! I'll turn my shoe radio into a loud speaker system. (*Up with the antenna.*) Testing, testing.... All right, everybody give me your attention, you must hear this message. Jesus is our Lord and Savior. Through Him we have forgiveness of sins and eternal life. He answers our prayers, and will be your closest friend, if you'll let Him. Got that? Good! Now that you've heard the message, spread it around! We can reach the world if we work together! This is secret agent Double-O-Alpha, over and out!

(*Alpha exits.*)

26.
Samson

(*The reporter enters.*)

REPORTER: Hello, and welcome to another edition of the Genesis Book of World Records. On today's exciting show we'll be meeting the world's strongest man. And we all know who that is, don't we? Wait a minute! I think I see him flying toward us now!

(*He looks up. Samson enters and looks up also.*)

SAMSON: What are you looking at up there?

REPORTER: Can't you see? Right up there! Is it a bird? Is it a plane?

SAMSON: It looks like Halley's Comet to me.

REPORTER: Oh. I guess you're right. I wonder where he is?

SAMSON: Where *who* is?

REPORTER: The world's strongest man. That's who we're waiting for.

SAMSON: But *I'm* the world's strongest man.

REPORTER: What? You are?

SAMSON: That's right.

REPORTER: But, but . . . I thought you'd be flying in!

SAMSON: No—I walked over.

REPORTER: Walked over? Wait a minute . . . Are you faster than a speeding bullet, more powerful than a locomotive, and able to leap tall buildings in a single bound?

SAMSON I don't know. I guess so. I've never tried.

REPORTER: Do you have wavy hair?

SAMSON: Yeah—I've got *long* wavy hair.

REPORTER: Do you have a girl friend who's a reporter?

SAMSON: You better believe it! She reports everything I do to the Philistines!

REPORTER: And does your name begin with an "S"?

SAMSON: Yes.

REPORTER: Then you're Superman! But where are your blue tights and red cape?

SAMSON: I'm not a souperman—I don't even like soup. I much prefer honey.

REPORTER: Well, if you're not Superman, who are you?

SAMSON: I'm the world's strongest man—my name's Samson.

REPORTER: And you're not from the planet Krypton?

SAMSON: Naw—I'm from Israel. Boy, you must get some strange people on this show.

REPORTER: If you're the world's strongest man, just what feats of strength have you done?

SAMSON: Well, one time I killed a lion with my bare hands. Another time I took on 1,000 men—and the only weapon I had was the jawbone of a donkey. And not a one of them was left standing when I was done! And then there was the time I tore off the gates of a city and carried them away.

REPORTER: Very impressive. You must work out a lot to build up your muscles.

SAMSON: Who needs muscles?

REPORTER: But where do you get your strength?

SAMSON: From the Lord.

REPORTER: I don't understand.

SAMSON: God gives me all my strength. I'm helpless by myself, but when the Spirit of the Lord comes upon me, I can move mountains out of the way—even throw them into the sea if necessary.

REPORTER: Amazing! Are there any limits to your strength?

SAMSON: I told you, it's not my strength, it's God's strength, and since it's God's strength, there's no limit to it.

REPORTER: Next to you, Superman would be a wimp. Can anyone have this strength?

SAMSON: God gives gifts and special endowments to people as He chooses, but it does say in the Bible that if we follow the Lord, He'll make sure our strength will never fail us, and that it will be renewed day by day.

REPORTER: Well, if I ever need any help, I'll be sure to give you a call.

SAMPSON: Don't call me—call the Lord!

REPORTER: Right you are. This is the Genesis Book of World Records . . . signing off.

(*The reporter and Samson exit.*)

27.
Catchy Camera

(*A man enters holding a wallet.*)

MAN: Wow! Look at this! Somebody lost a wallet. It was just lying here on the ground! I'll bet it fell out of somebody's pocket.... What's more, there's a ten-dollar bill inside! I'll bet if I looked further inside this wallet, I'd find the name and address of who it belonged to. I wonder what I should do? If I return the wallet, I might get a reward! But the reward would probably be only a dollar—if I got anything at all! On the other hand, if I keep the wallet, I'll have ten dollars for sure! (*He looks around.*) There's nobody around—who would know? I'm going to do it! I'm going to put the ten dollars in my pocket, and nobody will ever know! But wait! What will I do with the wallet? I can't return it now.... I know! I'll throw it in a trashcan! And no one will ever know!

(*Flunky pops up quickly.*)

FLUNKY: Hello there!

MAN: Aiiii! Who-who-who-who are you?!

FLUNKY: Sir, I want you to smile!

MAN: Smile?

FLUNKY: Yes! Because you're on—Catchy Camera!

MAN: Catchy Camera?!

FLUNKY: That's right! The hidden camera show that catches people when they least expect it! I'm Allen Flunky, and you see that tree over there?

MAN: Yes....

FLUNKY: Inside that tree is a television camera that's been filming your every move!

MAN: What?! Oh, no!

FLUNKY: That's right! Our viewing audience of seventy million people saw what you just did! And heard every word you said!

MAN: Oh, no!! I'm so embarrassed!

FLUNKY: Yes, all those people out there just saw you steal that money! Surprise! Surprise!

MAN: Here! I don't want it anymore!

FLUNKY: I'm sorry! It's too late now! We caught you in the act!

MAN (*embarrassed*): All of my friends watch this show! And my mother! Mom, I'm sorry!! Oh, why did I do it?

FLUNKY: You did it because you thought you could get away with it!

MAN: That's right! How was I to know that you'd be here watching me with your catchy camera?

FLUNKY: But, sir, don't you know that even if we hadn't been here, God would have seen what you did? God sees everything! No one can hide what they do from the Lord!

MAN: I forgot about the Lord seeing me!

FLUNKY: As it says in the Bible, your sin will find you out. And what is done in darkness will be revealed in the light.

MAN: I've certainly learned my lesson—the hard way!

FLUNKY: Good! (*Turns to address the audience*): Who will the *Catchy Camera* catch next? Don't let it be you!

(*The man and Flunky exit.*)

28.
Prodigal Son

(*Johnny enters.*)

JOHNNY: I'm bored. There's never anything to do around here.

(*Suzanne enters.*)

SUZANNE: Hey, Johnny! Hurry up and get ready for church! We're gonna be late!

JOHNNY: But I don't want to go.

SUZANNE: But today they'll be telling the story about the prodigal son.

JOHNNY: I've heard that story a hundred and fifty jillion times.

SUZANNE: Is that right?

JOHNNY: That's right.

SUZANNE: So I guess you know everything there is to know about it.

JOHNNY: That's right.

SUZANNE: Then tell it to me!

JOHNNY: What?

SUZANNE: Tell it to me! I'll bet you don't even know it!

JOHNNY: I do so!

SUZANNE: Then prove it!

JOHNNY: All right! I will ... Once upon a time there were two brothers ... One was named Bo, and one was named Luke.

(*Bo and Luke enter.*)

BO: Hi, I'm Bo.

LUKE: And I'm Luke.

JOHNNY: And they lived in a place called ... Gizzard County.

SUZANNE: What?! Oh, no! Here we go again!

JOHNNY: That's right. They were known as the Kooks of Gizzard.

SUZANNE: I don't believe it!

JOHNNY: Now Luke was a hard and faithful worker for his Uncle Jesse.

LUKE: I think I'll go plow the back forty and then clean the barn.

(*Luke exits.*)

JOHNNY: But Bo was a lazy, selfish loafer.

BO (*yawns*): I'm splitting this scene before they find something for me to do. I think I'll go cruising in my car, the General Grant.

(*Bo exits.*)

JOHNNY: One day Bo finally got fed up.

(*Bo and Uncle Jesse enter.*)

BO: Uncle Jesse, I'm fed up!

JESSE: I told you not to eat so much at supper, Bo.

BO: No, no! I mean I've had it up to here with this place. All we ever do around here is work, work, work....

JESSE: But it's an honest living, Bo. And your family is here.

BO: I don't care! There's got to be something better than this! I'm going to seek my fame

55

and fortune. Maybe I'll go to Hollywood and star in one of those dumb car chase shows—like *Miami Vice*.

JESSE: Oh, Bo, come to your senses, boy.

BO: I've made up my mind. But first I need my inheritance—that'll be enough to hold me over until I make my fortune.

(*BO and Jesse exit.*)

JOHNNY: So Uncle Jesse reluctantly gave Bo his inheritance, and Bo was on his way. But before Bo sought fame and fortune, he decided to live it up for a while. Unfortunately, Bo got so caught up with high living, that he soon ran out of all his inheritance.

(*Bo enters.*)

BO: Oh, no! It's gone! All my money is gone! I'm gonna have to find a job before I starve to death!

JOHNNY: But the only job Bo could find was for a mean, ole critter named Boss Pigg.

(*Boss Pigg the pig enters.*)

PIGG: I'm Boss Pigg. Now you listen here. I want you to clean out my pig pen, and if you do a good job, I'll let you eat some of the pig slop. But if you don't do a good job—you're not getting anything! Understand? (*Pigg exits.*)

JOHNNY: It was about this time that Bo finally came to his senses.

BO: Woe is me! I've done a terrible thing! I worked hard at home, but at least I had good meals there. I'm gonna go back and beg for forgiveness . . . and maybe Uncle Jesse will at least hire me as a worker—I'm sure he won't take me back as a nephew.

(*Bo exits.*)

JOHNNY: So Bo returned home. And when his Uncle Jesse saw him, he came running out to meet him.

(*Bo and Jesse enter from opposite directions.*)

JESSE: Bo! You've come home!

BO: Forgive me, Uncle Jesse. I've been foolish and selfish. I'm not worthy to be called your nephew.

JESSE: Bo! You just come with me! I'm giving you back a set of keys to the General Grant, and we're going to get Daisy and Luke and go celebrate! For you were lost in your own selfishness, but now you've found the truth!

(*Jesse and Bo exit.*)

JOHNNY: And they lived happily ever after in Gizzard County.

SUZANNE: Very interesting. And what's the moral of that story?

JOHNNY: Serve the Lord, because if you go your own way, you'll never find happiness.

SUZANNE: I see. . . . Now what were you saying about not going to church today?

JOHNNY: I see what you mean. Well, let's get going—I don't want to end up in some pig pen!

SUZANNE: All right! Let's go!

(*Johnny and Suzanne exit.*)

29.
Kooks of Gizzard

ANNOUNCER: Once upon a time there were two boys that lived in a place called Gizzard County. Their names were Bo Kook and Luke Kook. They were known as the Kooks of Gizzard.

(*Bo and Luke enter carrying a valentine card.*)

BO: Hi, I'm Bo!

LUKE: And I'm Luke!

ANNOUNCER: Now Bo and Luke were fun loving, good 'ole boys.

BO: Let's go for a ride in the General Grant!

LUKE: Okay, let's go!

(*Bo and Luke exit. We hear the sound of a car, which continues throughout the following exchange.*)

ANNOUNCER: Now most of Gizzard County was controlled by a mean old critter named Boss Pigg.

(*Boss Pigg the pig enters.*)

PIGG: I'm Boss Pigg—and don't you forget it!

ANNOUNCER: Now Boss Pigg didn't like the Kook boys.

PIGG: I'm gonna get me those Kook boys iffin it's the last thing I do Enos! Enos! Get over here!

(*Enos enters carrying a valentine card.*)

ENOS: Deputy Enos reporting for duty!

PIGG: Shut up! Can't you do something about those Kook boys?

ENOS: But, Boss, they always obey the law.

PIGG: What about all that noise they're making? Can't you arrest them for disturbing the peace?

ENOS: What?

PIGG (*screams*): I said, what about all that noise they're making? Can't you arrest them for disturbing the peace?

ENOS: I'm afraid you'll have to stop that shouting, Boss, or I'll have to arrest you for disturbing the peace.

PIGG: Enos, you cabbage brain!

ENOS: But, Boss—

PIGG: Shut up! Here come those Kook boys now.

(*The car sound ends. Bo and Luke enter.*)

BO: Howdy, Boss Pigg!

PIGG: Wait a minute! What's going on here? Why is everybody carrying a valentine?

ENOS: This is for my sweetheart, Daisy.

LUKE: This is for Daisy, too.

BO: And so's this one!

PIGG: Nobody ever sends *me* a valentine!

ENOS: That's because you're a mean, old, rotten crook.

LUKE: And a no-good, low-down, snake-in-the-grass.

BO: And a dishonest, good-for-nothing con man.

PIGG: I feel lower than a worm's belly.

LUKE: If you'd just change your ways, Boss, you'd be easier to like—and someone might send you a valentine someday.

PIGG: Aw, get outta here! All of you! I don't need you! And I don't need no valentines, neither!

(*Bo, Luke, and Enos exit.*)

PIGG: I can do just fine all by myself! Who needs friends, anyway?

(*Daisy enters carrying a valentine.*)

DAISY: You do, Boss Pigg. Everybody needs friends.

PIGG: Why, Daisy! What are you doing here?

DAISY: I'm here to give you this valentine, Boss.

PIGG: What?! Why are you giving *me* a valentine? I'm just a mean, old critter.

DAISY: Because when you have Jesus in your heart, you can love people who are unlovable!

PIGG: Daisy, you're prettier than a plate full of chicken gizzards!

DAISY: Boss, you say the sweetest things! You really could be a nice person if you tried.

PIGG: How can I be more lovable?

DAISY: What you need is a change of heart.

PIGG: You mean a heart transplant? Oh, no!

DAISY: No, Boss! I'm talking about a change of personality, a change of spirit and mind, as well as heart. It's called being born again. It's when Jesus takes over your life. He can take away all that meanness and dishonesty, clean up your life, and make you brand new!

PIGG: Daisy, you've won me over! I'm gonna change my ways! Where do I start?

DAISY: One of the ways to show Jesus you love Him is by loving others—like the Kook boys.

PIGG: All right, Daisy. Let's go find them!

DAISY: Now you're talking!

(*Daisy and Pigg exit.*)

ANNOUNCER: And that's the way they do things in Gizzard County.

30. Boss Pigg

(Daisy and Boss Pigg the pig enter from opposite directions.)

DAISY: Howdy, Boss Pigg!

PIGG: Well, well! If it isn't one of my favorite friends—Daisy Kook!

DAISY: What you been up to, Boss Pigg?

PIGG: Well, as a matter of fact, I just opened Gizzard County's first Mexican restaurant. I'm calling it Taco Piggs! Has a nice ring to it, don't you think?

DAISY: Boss, you're always building things or buying things. I think you own most of Gizzard County.

PIGG: That's right. And I won't be satisfied until I own it all!

DAISY: But why?

PIG Because I'm after fame, fortune, power, and popularity!

DAISY: And when you get all those things, do you think you'll really be satisfied?

PIGG: Probably not.

DAISY: Well then, what are some of your other goals?

PIGG: My main goal in life, my fondest wish, my ultimate dream, my greatest desire ... is to have a sausage named after me.

DAISY: A sausage?

PIGG: That's right! Jimmy Dean has his own sausage, Oscar Meyer has his sausage, Bob Evans has his sausage—why not a Boss Pigg sausage?

DAISY: That doesn't sound like a very great goal to me.

PIGG: Listen, Daisy, it would be much better for me to have a sausage *named* after me, than to be made *into* a sausage—iffin you know what I mean.

DAISY: I see what you mean.

PIGG: Besides, it would put my name in the history books—right alongside Colonel Sanders and Ronald McDonald.

DAISY: I'd rather have my name written in the Lamb's Book of Life.

PIGG: What's that?

DAISY: God has this great book in Heaven. Written inside are the names of all the Christians who have lived throughout the ages. Getting your name in there is much more important than having it in the history books.

PIGG: Why is that?

DAISY: Because human history is going to end and pass away. But whoever is written in the Lamb's Book of Life will live forever!

PIGG: How do you get your name in there? What great accomplishment do you have to do?

DAISY: All you have to do is accept Jesus as your Savior, obey His commandments, and seek His will in your life.

PIGG: Seek His will? You mean God cares about what I do to earn a living?

DAISY: Of course He does! Most people have goals in their life—some want to be doctors, or lawyers, or teachers, or computer experts—and that's all right—any honest work, that is honestly done is okay with God. What is most important is becoming the kind of *person* God wants you to be.

PIGG: But how do I know what God wants me to be?

DAISY: By studying His guidebook for our lives; the Bible. God has a wonderful plan for each of us. And if we follow it, we will be happy, fulfilled, productive people. However, even with all the things you've accomplished, Boss, you're not very happy, are you?

PIGG: I have to admit it, Daisy, you're right.

DAISY: What you need to do is turn your life over to Jesus, and let Him guide you. But you have to surrender *your* will in order to do *God's* will.

PIGG: But what if He asks me to do something I don't want to do?

DAISY: God created each of us with special gifts, talents, and desires. And His plan for us takes our likes and abilities into account. He knows what's best for us—if we will only believe that. God's plans for us are *good* plans. And you know what else?

PIGG: What?

DAISY: A lot of people who have turned their lives completely over to God have not only ended up in the Lamb's Book of life—but in the history books as well!

PIGG: I'll give it a try, Daisy! But where do I begin?

DAISY: Begin by reading the Bible. Soon the Lord will be talking to you about *your* life in particular.

PIGG: Maybe the Lord's got something better for me than giving my name to a greasy ole sausage ... I know! How about a ham? A Boss Pigg ham?

DAISY: Why, Boss, I've *always* thought you were a ham—and that's no baloney!

(*Daisy and Boss Pigg exit.*)

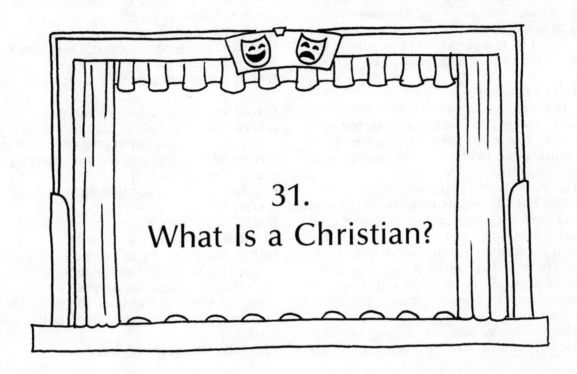

31.
What Is a Christian?

(*Daisy and Charlie enter from opposite directions.*)

CHARLIE: Hi, Daisy. How you doing? I was in the neighborhood and thought I would drop by.

DAISY: Well, well! If it ain't my ole friend Charlie from across the river in good ole Indie-I-anna! What brings you to the beautiful state of Kaintucky? Get tired of living in Hoosierland?

CHARLIE: Of course not!

DAISY: I understand the state of Indiana is also called the state of confusion. Ha! Ha! Ha!

CHARLIE: It is not!

DAISY: Well, all I can say is I'm proud to live in the great state of Kaintucky! The home of fast horses and beautiful women, Colonel Sanders, Daniel Boone, and the Kaintucky Wildcats!

CHARLIE: Wildcats! What kind of wildcats?

DAISY: *Big* wildcats! Some are almost seven feet tall!

CHARLIE: Oh, no!

DAISY: Don't worry! They only devour Hoosiers on the basketball court! Ha! Ha! Ha! Say, where did the name "Hoosier" come from, anyway?

CHARLIE: Oh, I know that! A long time ago there was a builder named Samuel Hoosier. He used to work in Kentucky a lot, but he would always hire Indiana work crews. The workers became known as "Hoosier's gang" and later, just "Hoosiers." Over the years, that name has come to mean anyone from Indiana.

DAISY: Well, what do you know about that? You learn something new ever day! I'll remember that the next time I play Trivial Pursuit! Now I've got another question for you.

CHARLIE: What?

DAISY: Just exactly what is a . . . Christian?

CHARLIE: Oh, that's easy! Everybody knows that!

DAISY: So . . . tell me!

CHARLIE: A Christian is . . . someone who goes to church.

DAISY: Not necessarily!

CHARLIE: Really? Well, what about a person who goes to church *and* Sunday school?

DAISY: Not always. It takes more than that to be a Christian.

CHARLIE: How about a person who does good deeds? Is that a Christian?

DAISY: You can do good deeds and not be a

Christian—but you're getting warmer!

CHARLIE: I've got it! A Christian is someone who believes in Jesus!

DAISY: Why, even the devil believes in Jesus! That doesn't make him a Christian!

CHARLIE: You've got a point there. Boy, I'm not sure anymore. Just what is a Christian?

DAISY: Well, I'll tell you. When you say you're a Christian, I reckon you've said a mouthful! Because to be a Christian means to be "Christ-like."

CHARLIE: Christ-like?

DAISY: That's right. A Christian is not only someone who accepts Jesus into their life, but who also walks like Jesus, talks like Jesus, forgives like Jesus, prays like Jesus, and who tries to do all things like Jesus did them.

CHARLIE: Wow! Is that really possible?

DAISY: No, but God wants us to try. Jesus was perfect, and He is our perfect example! God himself came down to live and walk on this earth in the form of a man. And that man was Jesus. He lived His life in such a way as to show us how to live ours. By following His example, we can have victorious, joy-filled, abundant life.

CHARLIE: You know, just like Samuel Hoosier, Jesus also had a hand-picked gang that worked with Him. Jesus' gang consisted of the twelve disciples.

DAISY: That's right! They were the *first* Christians!

CHARLIE: And now, all those who follow Jesus, like those first twelve disciples, can call themselves Christians too!

DAISY: Now you're getting it, Charlie!

CHARLIE: You sure are smart, Daisy. Are all Kentuckians so smart?

DAISY: When you compare them with Hoosiers they are.

CHARLIE: Now wait just a minute . . .

DAISY: I was just joshin! Can't you take a joke? Actually, the only smart people I know are the ones following Jesus. The rest don't have the brains of a crawdad!

CHARLIE: You can say that again! Uh, what's a crawdad?

DAISY: Why, that's a crayfish, of course!

CHARLIE: Oh! What's a crayfish?

DAISY: You poor city folks! You lead such sheltered lives! You just come along with me and I'll show you around. Maybe I'll even expose you to some of the finer things in life—like slopping the hogs and cleaning the chicken coop!

CHARLIE: Oh, boy! Let's go!

32. Giving

(*Daisy and Charlie enter from opposite directions.*)

DAISY: Well, lookee here. Don't tell me you are finally finished!

CHARLIE: Boy, Daisy, that was some job you gave me to do!

DAISY: All I asked you to do was mow the lawn.

CHARLIE: I know, but you've got five whole acres of grass!

DAISY: Aw, you're just soft from all that city living.

CHARLIE: Well, if I'd known it was going to be so hard, I would have asked for more than ten dollars.

DAISY: You just need some grit, Charlie. And one way to get grit is to eat grits, so come on inside and I'll fix you a bowl and give you your money.

CHARLIE: Okay!

DAISY: I guess you'll be giving a dollar of that to the Lord.

CHARLIE: What? What for?

DAISY: Why, Charlie, don't you tithe?

CHARLIE: What's that?

DAISY: That's giving one-tenth of what you make to the Lord's work.

CHARLIE: But it's only a dollar.

DAISY: The amount doesn't matter. Everybody needs to do their part so the local church and God's program can keep going. Churches have bills too, you know.

CHARLIE; But God has everything—He's rich. Why does He need my money?

DAISY: Because more often than not, God works through people.

CHARLIE: But I worked hard for that ten dollars! Why should I give God ten percent? He wasn't out there pushing that lawn mower.

DAISY: But He gave you the health and strength to work, didn't He, as well as the job opportunity? Besides, giving back to God helps you develop a character more like God's. God is *always* giving. He even gave His only Son to die for our sins. Also, whenever you give, that gives God seed to work with.

CHARLIE: Seed? My money is seed?

DAISY: That's right. If you want a harvest of corn, you have to plant seed corn. You can't get a harvest of anything unless you first plant a seed.

CHARLIE: So, if I plant my money in the work of God, it acts as a seed to bring me a harvest of financial blessing?

DAISY: Right! It's a fixed law of God, by crackie! Whatever you sow, you're going to reap. And if you sow nothing, you'll reap nothing.

CHARLIE: But what if you don't have any money to plant? Does that mean you're going to be poor?

DAISY: Not necessarily. The most important thing you can plant is *yourself*. Your total self. Your time, your talent, your prayers, your faith—everything. Make your life a seed—give God everything—and then you can really reap a harvest of blessings.

CHARLIE: Wait a minute! You mean I'm going to have to dig a hole and bury myself like a seed?

DAISY: No, Charlie. That's what being baptized is all about. When you are submerged in water—and that's what the word "baptism" means—you are symbolically buried. Your old self dies and your new life begins—that's being born again!

CHARLIE: But I have so little to give.

DAISY: That's what you think now! A tiny little seed is all it takes to produce the biggest tree. Who knows what God will be able to produce in your life? Remember the story in the Bible about the little boy with the five loaves and two fish?

CHARLIE: Five loaves! That's a lot of bread!

DAISY: Not really. In those days a loaf was like a little bun or pancake—so we're really talking about just enough for himself. Anyway, he gave what he had to the Lord, and the Lord multiplied it so that his little lunch fed thousands of people!

CHARLIE: And if the Lord can do that with a little, think of what He can do with a lot! Oh, boy! Do you have any other jobs I could do for you?

DAISY: Why sure! There's always work to be done on a farm! We can start by milking the cows, slopping the hogs, stacking the hay, cleaning the chicken coop, and painting the barn—and then we can move on to the hard stuff.

CHARLIE: On second thought, I think I'll go look for work in the city. You don't need me here—you need Rambo!

DAISY: Who's Rambo?

CHARLIE: He's a guy who's a lot tougher than I am!

DAISY: Well, if he's looking for work, send him on by!

CHARLIE: I'll be sure and tell him if I happen to see him. Ha! Ha! Ha!

(*Charlie exits.*)

DAISY: That poor, soft city boy. Well, maybe this Rambo critter will be by. I'll get the paint ready for the barn just in case.

(*Daisy exits.*)

33.
The Kook Family

(Daisy and Charlie enter.)

CHARLIE: Boy, Daisy, you sure have a big farm!

DAISY: Yep! And it's been in my family for generations, Charlie. Why, Gizzard County was even founded by one of my ancestors, that famous pioneer, Davy Kookette.

CHARLIE: Do you have any other famous relatives?

DAISY: Why sure! There are many famous Kooks throughout history! There was General Ulysses S. Kook who fought in the Civil War. And there was Leonardo Da Kooci, the famous I-talian inventor. He invented freeze-dried spaghetti. And there was Orville and Wilbur Kook. They were the first men to fly in Gizzard County when their still blew up! And who could forget that famous western outlaw, Billy the Kook?

CHARLIE: Wow! You've got quite a family history!

DAISY: You ain't heard nothing yet! My most famous relatives include Abraham, Isaac, Jacob, Jeremiah, Moses, King David, and Elijah!

CHARLIE: Wow! You're related to all those people in the Bible? Really?

DAISY: That's right! And so are you!

CHARLIE: No I'm not!

DAISY: Yes you are! When you became a Christian, God adopted you into His Family. That means you're a brother to Jesus Christ, and through His blood you became a blood relative to all those great men of God!

CHARLIE: Well, we all come from Adam and Eve, so in a sense we're all related anyway—even though my teacher at school says that the Garden of Eden was a myth and that we're all descended from monkeys.

DAISY: Now hold on! There may be lots of Kooks in my family, but there's no gorillers! If you ask me, evolution is mind pollution!

CHARLIE: That's right. My Father is the Lord—not King Kong!

DAISY: And one of the great things about having God as a Father and Jesus as a brother is that we become joint sharers and joint heirs to all the promises and inheritance of God.

CHARLIE: What does that mean?

DAISY: Everything that God promised to Abraham and his descendants comes right on down to us. We can claim all those blessings of God in the name of Jesus—iffin we have the right motives, of course, and give God time to work.

CHARLIE: What kind of blessings?

DAISY: All kinds of blessings! Blessings of health, prosperity, protection, peace, joy, love—and a great inheritance to come in Heaven. Really, all that God has is ours—it says that in the parable of the prodigal son.

CHARLIE: How do I find out how to get some of these promised blessings?

DAISY: Just read your Bible! It's full of them, from beginning to end!

CHARLIE: Wow!

DAISY: And you know something else? When you're born, you always have some of the characteristics of your earthly father—you may look like him, talk like him, and have a lot of the same personality.

CHARLIE That's right. I do.

DAISY: Well, when you're born again, God the Father starts working inside of you with the Holy Spirit, and pretty soon you have many of the same characteristics of your *heavenly* Father.

CHARLIE: Really?

DAISY: That's right. You may begin to look like Him as the glory of the Lord shines on your face, talk like Him as you begin to tell others about Jesus, and even display His personality as you become more loving, giving, kind, and compassionate.

CHARLIE: You're right, Daisy. There has been a big change in the way I act since I became a follower of Jesus.

DAISY: You know what, Charlie? I understand you once looked up your Family tree ... and found out you were the *sap!* Ha! Ha! Ha!

CHARLIE: Now wait just a minute!

DAISY: I was just joshin! You city folks sure are touchy! Hey, you're staying for supper, aren't you?

CHARLIE: What are you having?

DAISY: We're having catfish fiddlers, brain sandwiches, and burgoo.

CHARLIE: Burgoo? What's burgoo?

DAISY: It's from an old family recipe passed down for generations! It's chicken, pork, wild rabbit, squirrel, and deer meat in a soup so thick you can cement bricks with the leftovers!

CHARLIE: I think I'll pass.

DAISY: Are you sure? It'll stick to your ribs!

CHARLIE: That's what I'm afraid of!

(*Daisy and Charlie exit.*)

34.
Girls Just Want to Have Fun

(Daisy and Stacey enter.)

DAISY: Well, Stacey, how do you like the country so far?

STACEY: Like wow, Daisy, I don't know if I'm really cut out for country living. Like, what a bummer. For sure.

DAISY: What's wrong with it?

STACEY: Oh, it's all right for some people, but for me, it's dull. Really dull to the max. Like "Hee Haw" city!

DAISY: So what's so great about living in a big town?

STACEY: Oh, it's totally awesome. I like the excitement of the city. The flash and sparkle and glitter. Cruising the streets with your friends. Listening to the jammin' music. The only music you have to listen to around here is made by crickets.

DAISY: There are a lot of exciting things to do in the country. Why, every Saturday night we have a hootenanny!

STACEY: What's a hootenanny?

DAISY: About the same as a hoedown.

STACEY: So what's a hoedown?

DAISY: You know—a jamboree!

STACEY: Like wow, Daisy, I think we need a translator. Surely there's someone around here who knows val talk.

DAISY: You know, I can't understand why you don't like it out here. You call yourself a valley girl. Well, we have lots of valleys around here. Only, we call them hollers. So I guess in country talk you'd be called a holler girl! Ha! Ha! Ha!

STACEY: Gruesome to the max!

DAISY: Aw, just give country living a chance. It'll grow on you!

STACEY: You know what, Daisy? I'm kind of afraid of being a Christian for some of the same reasons. For sure.

DAISY: What do you mean?

STACEY: Christians just can't have any fun. Everything is a sin but Putt-Putt golf, and even that's a sin if you do it on Sunday.

DAISY: Well, I will admit that some Christians walk around with such a serious and sour look on their face that they look like they've been baptized in vinegar and weaned on a dill pickle!

STACEY: Is it a sin to want to have a little fun? Like Cyndi Lauper says, "Girls just want to have fun!" Is that so bad?

DAISY: Of course not! But who's Cyndi Lauper? Is she your Sunday-school teacher?

STACEY: Oh, no! She's a singer with orange hair.

DAISY: Orange hair?! That poor girl! What kind of disease would cause that?

STACEY: That's just the way she likes to wear it!

DAISY: You city folks are really strange sometimes. But getting back to your question, Christians are supposed to live their lives in moderation and not go totally wild, because we're supposed to be an example to the world. But we should also be the most fun-filled and joy-filled people around.

STACEY: We should?

DAISY: That's right! Because we have reasons to celebrate all the time! Just think, God has promised to meet our every need if we lean on Him, and He's given us eternal life to boot!

STACEY: But what can I do to have fun as a Christian? What's right and what's wrong?

DAISY: I don't think it matters so much *what* you do, as *why* you do it. God didn't give us a bunch of rules and regulations to tie us down, but to set us free. He knows that certain things just aren't good for us, and He guides us in His Word as to what these things are. When you go driving, you obey the traffic laws, don't you?

STACEY: For sure!

DAISY: Traffic laws are set up to keep us from getting hurt. The same is true with God's laws.

STACEY: Totally cosmic to the max. But ... can I still go to parties?

DAISY: Life can't be *all* fun and games—there's a serious side to life, so there needs to be a balance. But just think, as a Christian you can have good, clean fun with a clear conscience.

STACEY: For sure.

DAISY: Just remember: there's pleasure in sin for a season, but the world is partying on a sinking ship. And one day, the party for them will end in tragedy. But for Christians, by obeying the Lord, our joy and happiness will last forever.

STACEY: Like, maybe I'll give being a Christian another chance. And maybe I'll even give country living another chance.

DAISY: Now you're talking, by crackie! So let's get on with the grand tour!

STACEY: All right! Let's go!

(*Daisy and Stacey exit.*)

35.
Sowing and Reaping

(*Daisy and Stacey enter.*)

STACEY: Like wow, this place is totally awesome to the max. For sure.

DAISY: Is this your first trip to the country, Stacey?

STACEY: For sure. Like, you have so much space out here. It's blowing my mind.

DAISY: That's the way we like it—wide-open spaces.

STACEY: Like, what is that I smell?

DAISY: It's called "fresh air."

STACEY: Wow, I've never smelled that before. I'm used to exhaust fumes.

DAISY: If you like to smell things, I'll take you out to the barn sometime and give you a *real* thrill! Ha! Ha! Ha!

STACEY: You're far out, Daisy. For sure.

DAISY: You sure do talk funny.

STACEY: It's called "valley talk." Like it's sooooo cool. Really with it. To the max.

DAISY: Whatever you say. I think I'll stick with country talk.

STACEY: Like, what do you do for entertainment around here? Is there a bonerama nearby? We could go full-sesh with Pac-Man or Space Invaders.

DAISY: What's a ... bonerama?

STACEY: You know; a shopping mall!

DAISY: There's not a shopping mall within fifty miles of here. And nary a general store either.

STACEY: Wow. Like primitive city. Like, where do you get your food?

DAISY: We grow it mostly. We grow a lot of what we eat.

STACEY: Wow, like totally organic. What do you grow?

DAISY: All kinds of things: corn, greens, soybeans, mango peppers, carrots, melons ...

STACEY: Far out. Like, how do you grow stuff like that anyway?

DAISY: Well, Genesis tells us that all plants produce seeds after their own kind. All we have to do is take those seeds and plant them in the ground. If you want melons, you plant melon seeds. If you want peppers, you plant pepper seeds. You reap—that is, you harvest—whatever you sow into the ground.

STACEY: Like ... wow!

DAISY: And you know what? The same is true in your life. One of God's most basic laws is that you harvest what you sow. If you sow lots of love toward other people, they'll respond in a loving way towards you. If you're friendly, you'll have lots of friends. And if you're kind and giving, God will influence people to be kind and giving towards you.

STACEY: Like, totally cosmic.

DAISY: But, on the other hand, if you're a mean 'ole critter, people will act the same way towards you. So you have to watch yourself, and follow after Jesus and *His* example for living.

STACEY: Like, I'm beginning to see what you mean. For sure.

DAISY: Speaking of food, can you stay for dinner?

STACEY: Like what are you having?

DAISY: Just a typical country dinner: collard greens and fatback, grits, chitlins, blackeyed peas, and corn pone!

STACEY: Wow! Like, could you at least throw in a Twinky? At least I would know what that is!

DAISY: Why sure, but in the meantime, how about a tour of the farm?

STACEY: All right. Let's go for it!

DAISY: I'll make a country girl out of you yet, Stacey!

STACEY: Like wow! Is there an official country girl handbook I can follow?

DAISY: No. But don't worry. By the time you get back home, you'll be so country, everyone you meet will think you been picked from a corn field.

STACEY: Awesome to the max....

(*Daisy and Stacey exit.*)

36.
Lost and Found

(Daisy enters.)

DAISY: Well, well, it looks like it's going to be another quiet country day—just like I like them!

(José enters.)

JOSÉ: Hola! Hola! (Pronounced, "ola.")

DAISY: What in the world?

JOSÉ: Buenos dias!

DAISY: Say, what? Who are you?

JOSÉ: My name is José.

DAISY: You're not from around here, are you?

JOSÉ: No—I'm from south of the border.

DAISY: You mean, Tennessee?

JOSÉ: No, no—I'm from Mexico!

DAISY: What are you doing in these parts?

JOSÉ: I'm just passing through on my way to San José.

DAISY: I think you made a wrong turn somewhere. This is Gizzard County, Kentucky.

JOSÉ: Is that in the United States?

DAISY: Why sure! Boy, you *are* lost, aren't you?

JOSÉ: Not as lost as I used to be! Before I found Jesus, I was wondering through life without any direction or purpose at all. I was just bouncing off whatever happened to me! But since I found the Lord, I know where I'm going and what I'm supposed to be doing!

DAISY: I know what you mean.

JOSÉ: And if I happen to take a wrong turn, I know the Lord will lead me back on the right track! And what is your name, senorita?

DAISY: My name's Daisy. Daisy Kook.

JOSÉ: What a marvelous name! And you look marvelous too!

DAISY: Why, thank you.

JOSÉ: But more important than looking marvelous is feeling marvelous. And the only way to really feel marvelous is with Jesus in your heart.

DAISY: Yes, I know.

JOSÉ: And isn't this just a marvelous day? A marvelous day to look and feel marvelous!

DAISY: I suppose so.

JOSÉ: Every day can be a marvelous day if you have Jesus as the Lord of your life.

DAISY: But does that mean that every day will be free from worry and trouble?

JOSÉ: No, no. But you'll have someone helping you *out* of those worries and troubles. As it says in the Bible, "Many are the afflictions of the righteous, but the Lord delivers him out of them all." Isn't that absolutely marvelous?

DAISY: You're quite a marvelous fellow, aren't you?

JOSÉ: That's because the Lord inside of me is marvelous, and all that marvelousness comes out. So you see, anyone who is a Christian can be truly marvelous.

DAISY: Well, I'm a Christian.

JOSÉ: Isn't that marvelous! The Lord brings Christians together when we least expect it! I needed a helping hand, and the Lord led me to you! You know, the Lord will lead us day by day if we ask Him to.

DAISY: You're right, José; sometimes the Lord has helped me through a Christian friend, or spoken to my heart during a sermon, or guided me with a scripture. He's trying to talk to us all the time, if we'll take the time to listen.

JOSÉ: So tell me, do you know the way to San José?

DAISY: I don't think you can get there from here. Maybe if you backed up to Texas and took a left instead of a right.

JOSÉ: Aaaaiii! Maybe that's where I went wrong! Isn't that marvelous?

DAISY: Why is that marvelous?

JOSÉ: Because if I hadn't taken that wrong turn, I would never have met such a marvelous person as you! You see, Jesus can even take our mistakes and make them into something marvelous.

DAISY: It does say in the Bible, "all things work together for good for those who love God."

JOSÉ: So really, we can't lose! God has everything under control. Well, I'd better be on my way! It was nice meeting you, senorita! Adios!

DAISY: And a mucho bye-o to you, too!

(Daisy and José exit.)

37.
The Family of God

(Daisy and Suzanne enter.)

SUZANNE: Well, if it isn't my old friend Daisy Kook! How you doing, Daisy?

DAISY: Mighty fine! Mighty fine! Couldn't be better! What brings a city girl like you all the way to Gizzard County, Suzanne?

SUZANNE: I'm doing a research paper for school on country living. And since you're the only one I know who lives in the country, I've come to ask you some questions.

DAISY: Well, you've come to the right person! I'm as country as hot biscuits and apple butter, cowboy boots, old pick-up trucks, and homemade quilts. So fire away!

SUZANNE: The first thing I'd like to know is, is it true that country folks are very friendly?

DAISY: Sure enough.

SUZANNE: Why is that?

DAISY: Well, around here, it's mainly because everybody's related.

SUZANNE: Related?

DAISY: That's right. I'm surrounded by aunts, uncles, brothers, sisters, parents, grandparents, great grandparents, nieces, nephews, first cousins, second cousins, third cousins, country cousins....

SUZANNE: What's a country cousin?

DAISY: They are the people who show up at a family reunion and partake of all the food—but nobody knows who they are. So we just call them country cousins and let it go at that.

SUZANNE: That's mighty friendly, all right.

DAISY: That's the way country folks are.

SUZANNE: I sure envy you. You come from such a big family and they all live near by! In the city, what little family I have is spread out so far, we hardly ever see each other.

DAISY: Why, Suzanne, you're a part of the biggest family in the world!

SUZANNE: What do you mean?

DAISY: You've got more brothers and sisters than the Brady Bunch, the Huxtables, and the Keatons put together!

SUZANNE: No I don't!

DAISY: Yes you do! And your family stretches across the country and around the world!

SUZANNE: What are you talking about, Daisy?

DAISY: That's the way it is, Suzanne, when you belong to the family of God!

SUZANNE: What?

DAISY: God is our Father. And all Christians everywhere are brothers and sisters. Christianity isn't just a religion, it's a family and we're supposed to love one another, and share each other's warmth and friendship.

SUZANNE: I see what you mean!

DAISY: The people in the world don't know what they're missing. There are many hurting, lonely, seemingly forgotten, and abandoned people out there. If these people would just come to the heavenly Father, who loves them very much, and seek out a church that believes in true Christian fellowship, their lives could be transformed!

SUZANNE: That's beautiful, Daisy.

DAISY: And just think, one day we'll be with our Father in Heaven, living forever and ever with all our brothers and sisters who have lived throughout the ages! What a wonderful family to be a part of.

SUZANNE: That's the truth!

DAISY: And speaking of families, I've got a great idea!

SUZANNE: What?

DAISY: Instead of you asking me all those questions, why don't I introduce you to some of my kinfolk—and you can get a real sampling of country life.

SUZANNE: That is a great idea!

DAISY: Let's see. Besides me, there's my brothers, Bo Kook and Luke Kook and Uncle Jesse Kook, and Moe Kook, Larry Kook, and Curly Kook, Stanley Kook and Ollie Kook, John-boy Kook and Mary-Ellen Kook ...

SUZANNE: I get the idea.

DAISY: And we can't leave out Groucho, Harpo, and Chico Kook, Sheriff Kook, and Mayor Kook, Duke Kook, Spanky Kook, Alfalfa Kook, and Buckwheat Kook....

SUZANNE: All right, already!

DAISY: Yep, there sure are a lot Kooks in Gizzard County.

SUZANNE: And you're one of them!

(Daisy and Suzanne exit.)

38.
The Names of God

(Daisy and Suzanne enter.)

SUZANNE: You know what, Daisy?

DAISY: What?

SUZANNE: You sure have a pretty name.

DAISY: Why thank you!

SUZANNE: Why did your parents give you that name?

DAISY: Because when they first saw me, they just knew I was going to be wild as the hills.

SUZANNE: And they were right!

DAISY: So they named me after a wildflower—a Daisy.

SUZANNE: I see.

DAISY: You know, all names have meanings.

SUZANNE: They do?

DAISY: That's right. Don't you know that you are named after a flower, too?

SUZANNE: I am?

DAISY: Sure! Suzanne comes from the Spanish name Suzanna—which means "lily"!

SUZANNE: Wow! I didn't know that!

DAISY: Yep! We've got a regular garden growing here! Ha! Ha! Ha!

SUZANNE: You know, it's amazing how parents seem to know how their children are going to turn out, and they instinctively pick names that really match their children's personalities.

DAISY: That's so true, Suzanne! Like take some of my relatives for example. There's Marco Polo Kook—he likes to travel, and Johann Sebastian Kook—he plays the pie-anner and fiddle, and Captain James T. Kook—he's an asternut.

SUZANNE: That's amazing.

DAISY: Yeah. And there's Vincent Van Kook—he likes to paint. In fact, he painted our barn just the other day.

SUZANNE: I get the idea.

DAISY: And there's Dr. Livingston Kook—a missionary in Kukamonga, and Kareem Abdul Ja-Kook, the basketball player—otherwise known as Dr. K.

SUZANNE: All right already! You sure have a strange—I mean, interesting—family.

DAISY: I'll bet you know what "Jesus" means.

SUZANNE: Sure. Jesus means "savior" and "deliverer." He was given that name by God the Father because He was going to be the savior of our souls, right?

DAISY: Yep! Jesus doesn't just save our souls! He saves our minds, our emotions, our lives, our families, our finances, delivers us from sickness, fear, mental problems, sin, addictions, heartbreak, loneliness, anxiety, oppression, depression, obsessions. . . .

SUZANNE: If ever there was a name that accurately described someone—it's "Jesus"!

DAISY: Ain't it the truth! And Jesus was also called Immanuel, which means "God with us," because He is with us all the time. And He is also called Jehovah, which means "I am that I am."

SUZANNE: What does that mean?

DAISY: It means that He can be anything He wants to be—or anything we need Him to be. And He's also called "Wonderful, Counselor, the Prince of Peace, the Mighty God, and the Everlasting Father!"

SUZANNE: The Lord is certainly a great God!

DAISY: And the best part is—Jesus left us His name. Christians are people that can use the name of Jesus to take authority over situations, to command mountains of problems to move out of the way, to set people free, and to pray and get results and answers!

SUZANNE: You're so right!

DAISY: And I'll tell you something else especially for you. He is also called "The Lily of the Valley!" So when ever you get in a valley, Suzanne/Lily, you can join that other lily and He'll walk right by your side!

SUZANNE: Well, praise the Lord!

DAISY: You know, speaking of names, when girls get married they take the last names of their husbands.

SUZANNE: That's right.

SUZANNE: Well, I sure will miss being a Kook.

SUZANNE: I don't think you have to worry, Daisy—you'll *always* be a kook!

(Daisy and Suzanne exit.)

39. Buford T. Mule

(*Daisy and Buford the mule enter from opposite directions.*)

DAISY: Well, if it ain't Buford T. Mule! How you doing, Buford?

BUFORD: Not so good.

DAISY: What's wrong?

BUFORD: I'll tell you what's wrong! I'm tired of being a gopher!

DAISY: Why, you're not a gopher! You're a mule!

BUFORD: No I'm not! I'm a gopher! I go for this! And go for that! And have to do this, and have to do that. And I'm tired of it!

DAISY: What are you talking about?

BUFORD: When I was young, my parents used to tell me to do this and do that. Then my teachers told me to do this and do that. And now my employer tells me to do this and do that! And I'm getting tired of being told what to do! In fact, I'm starting to get positively stubborn!

DAISY: Well, it's part of a mule's nature to be stubborn.

BUFORD: But I don't want to be stubborn! And I don't want to be told what to do all the time. I'd like to be a free mule for a change.

DAISY: Why, Jesus can make you free!

BUFORD: Oh, no He can't! I know all about that religious stuff. If I came to the Lord, then *He* would tell me to do this and do that, and not to do this and not to do that—just like everybody else only more so.

DAISY: Buford, you're really mistaken. You've got the wrong idea of what God is like. God isn't looking for slaves—God's looking for sons and daughters. A lot of people think God is demanding and mean, and that's just not true!

BUFORD: It isn't?

DAISY: Of course not! God is love! And He wants your love more than anything else. And to know Jesus is to love Him. And when you're in love with someone, you *want* to do things for him.

BUFORD: But how can Jesus make me free from all the other demands on my life?

DAISY: Jesus said, "Come to me, all you who labor and are heavy laden, and I will give you rest." With God's love living and growing in our hearts, we'll just naturally want to serve others. And God will see to it that we get the rest we need—and also the joy.

BUFORD: Joy?

DAISY: That's right. God is concerned about our happiness. All work and no play would make anyone depressed.

BUFORD: Maybe the Lord will make me rich so I don't have to work.

DAISY: I kind of doubt that, Buford ole buddy. It says in the Bible that we're all expected to work for a living. But the Lord can sure *ease* our burdens, and even make us more prosperous than we could make ourselves.

BUFORD: But what about all those rules and regulations and laws and commandments in the Bible?

DAISY: When God our Father tells us to do something, it's always for our own good. He's trying to lead us into an abundant life, and we have to cooperate by applying His guidelines for living. For example, the Bible says, be good to your neighbors and you'll have better neighbors, by crackie!

BUFORD: *That's* in the Bible?

DAISY: Well, words to that effect. That's from the Daisy Kook Kaintucky paraphrased version of the Bible! Ha! Ha! Ha!

BUFORD: Maybe you're right, Daisy. I need to stop grumbling and complaining and start doing things God's way!

DAISY: Atta boy, Buford! By the way, are you heading into town?

BUFORD: I don't know. Why?

DAISY: How about giving me a ride?

BUFORD: See there! Now *you're* telling me what to do!

DAISY: Sorry about that, Buford ole buddy. I love you too much to put you out of your way.

BUFORD: Oh, that's okay, Daisy. I reckon I love you too. And that's why I'd be more than happy to give you a ride into town. So just hop on my back and away we'll go.

DAISY: All right! Hiyo, Buford, away!

(Daisy and Buford exit.)

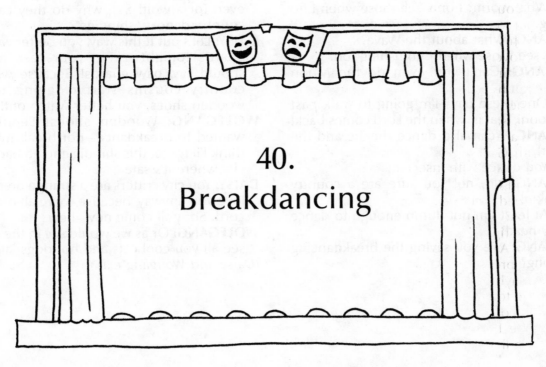

40.
Breakdancing

(Daisy enters.)

DAISY: It sure is a beautiful day! I sure love the country—with its bright sunshine, rolling green hills, and the sweet sounds of nature! (We hear a howl.) What in the world was that?

(Wolfgang the wolf enters.)

WOLFGANG: Hello there, you country cutie! What's happening?

DAISY: Well, I'll be switched! You're the first UFO I've ever seen!

WOLFGANG: UFO?

DAISY: Unidentified Furry Object.

WOLFGANG: I'm not a furry object! I'm a wolf!

DAISY: You don't look like any wolf I've ever seen!

WOLFGANG: That's because I'm a city wolf!

DAISY: You're not after my chickens, are you? Iffin you are, I'll have to get the shotgun!

WOLFGANG: No, no! The only chickens I eat are Colonel Sander's original recipe!

DAISY: Then what are you doing out here in the country?

WOLFGANG: My name is Wolfgang von Wolff, and I'm here for the dance contest.

DAISY: Dance contest? You mean the one they're having at the shindig?

WOLFGANG: What's a shindig?

DAISY: That's a hootenanny, a jamboree, a hoedown, and a square dance all rolled into one!

WOLFGANG: Then that must be the place. I understand first prize is a guest appearance on "Hee Haw"!

DAISY: That's right. And you'd fit right in with those dancing pigs!

WOLFGANG: Listen, I'll have you know I'm the Michael Jackson of the animal kingdom! I've got natural rhythm and style!

DAISY: You've also got four feet! That should give you an unfair advantage! Just what kind of dancing do you do?

WOLFGANG: Breakdancing.

DAISY: Breakdancing? What do you break?

WOLFGANG: Hopefully, nothing.

DAISY: Then why is it called "breakdancing"?

WOLFGANG: Because you spin around on your head, twirl on your hands, twist on your shoulders, and bounce on your stomach—you break all the rules!

DAISY: I hope you've got good medical insurance.

WOLFGANG: Haven't you ever seen breakdancing? Surely you've seen the Worm.

DAISY: What worm? I only see those when I go fishing.

WOLFGANG: What about the Wave?

DAISY: I see those when I go fishing too.

WOLFGANG: Can't you even do the Moon Walk?

DAISY: One these days I'm going to walk *past* the moon! That is, when the Lord comes back!

WOLFGANG: I can also dance the Tic and the Spider!

DAISY: You dance with insects?

WOLFGANG: No, no! You sure are a country bumpkin!

DAISY: At least I'm not dumb enough to dance on my head!

WOLFGANG: Are you saying the breakdancing is wrong?

DAISY: There's nothing wrong with any kind of dancing—as long as it's done in a decent and modest manner and if it's done as unto the Lord.

WOLFGANG: What do you mean?

DAISY: It says in the Bible, everything you do in word or deed, do all as unto the Lord, and in the name of Jesus. So be careful when you're following the latest fads and doing the latest dance step—make sure the Lord would be pleased with what you're doing.

WOLFGANG: Don't worry, I never get too wild—even for a wolf! Say, why do they call these country dances "shindigs"?

DAISY: Let's put it this way, you better wear shin guards tonight—or in your case maybe I should say, paw guards! Because when my country cousins start clogging in their wooden shoes, you better watch out!

WOLFGANG: Wooden shoes! Eeeiiioow! I wanted to breakdance—not break my feet! I think I'll forget this shindig and go back to the city where it's safe.

DAISY: You city critters are a strange breed, but I love you anyway, because we're all one in the Lord. So, y'all come now, hear?

WOLFGANG: Or as we would say in the city—I'll see all you cool cats and hot dogs later!

(*Daisy and Wolfgang exit.*)

41. Big City Blues

(*Buford the mule enters.*)

BUFORD: Wow, the city sure is a big place—I guess that's why they call it the "big" city. And all that noise—I guess that's what they call noise pollution. You just never know what you're going to see or hear. (*Wolfgang the wolf howls offstage.*) Now what was that?

(*Wolfgang enters.*)

WOLFGANG: That was me! Hello there, stranger. You're not from around here, are you?

BUFORD: As a matter of fact, I ain't.

WOLFGANG: I thought so. You just didn't *fit in* with everybody else.

BUFORD: Who are you?

WOLFGANG: I'm Wolfgang von Wolff.

BUFORD: Well, howdy. I'm Buford T. Mule.

WOLFGANG: Happy to make your acquaintance.

BUFORD: Are you a real live city person?

WOLFGANG: I'm a real live city wolf.

BUFORD: What's a wolf doing in the city?

WOLFGANG: There are lots of wolves in the city. And some of them wear sheep's clothing—so you better watch out. As for me, I prowl the concrete jungle. The city streets are my domain.

BUFORD: You sure do dress funny. Do all city folks dress that strange?

WOLFGANG: Strange?! It's called being in style!

BUFORD: I don't know. You wouldn't find that in a Dollar General store.

WOLFGANG: Listen, I'm Mr. Cool. I'm so cool I wear sweaters in the summer time. I make Eddie Murphy look like one of the Beverly Hillbillies!

BUFORD: Well I'll be switched.

WOLFGANG: So what brings you to the city?

BUFORD: Just visiting. I've heard so much about city life, I just had to come and see it for myself.

WOLFGANG: Well, there's certainly lots to see— the bright lights, the fast living, the crowds of people. But if you're going to stay long, you're going to need some lessons on how to be cool.

BUFORD: Can't I just buy an air conditioner?

WOLFGANG: No, no! Not that kind of cool. I'm talking about a state of mind. Like, having everything under control. You know what I mean?

BUFORD: Not really.

WOLFGANG: Like, take your name, for instance.

BUFORD: My name?

WOLFGANG: You're going to have to change it. Buford T. Mule is too square. You need a strong, macho nickname. How about Rocky Shagg?

BUFORD: I'm not going to change my name! And I don't care about being cool either.

WOLFGANG: But you've got to be like the "in" crowd—with the latest fashions, the latest music, the latest fads—or you'll be a social outcast. The most important thing in life is being popular—blending in with the crowd.

BUFORD: I'd rather be the unique person that God made me. I think being myself is more important than trying to be like everybody else!

WOLFGANG: Listen, you need to do something about your clothes. You need to buy the latest styles—no matter what the cost!

BUFORD: Sound kind of dumb to me. What's wrong with overalls, jeans, and flannel shirts?

WOLFGANG: They're not flashy enough! You've got to "get it together."

BUFORD: But I've got it together—in Jesus.

WOLFGANG: But you've got to "fit in"!

BUFORD: I fit in with Jesus—that's what counts. I try to accommodate people all I can—up to a point. But I'm not going to be a carbon copy of everybody else.

WOLFGANG: Well, you've got guts, I'll give you that. It takes courage to be yourself these days—and not be part of the "in" crowd.

BUFORD: Look at it this way; man was not made in man's image—man was made in God's image. So we should all be ourselves, and try to be like Jesus, God's perfect example.

WOLFGANG: I see what you mean.

BUFORD: Say, since you're from around here, could you show me some of the local hot spots?

WOLFGANG: Sure. As a matter of fact, I know this place down on Main Street ... that has absolutely no shade at all! It's a *real* hot spot!

BUFORD: Well doggies! What are we waiting for? Let's go!

(*Buford and Wolfgang exit.*)

43.
Family Feud

(*Daisy enters.*)

DAISY: What a beautiful day. That's one thing I really like about the country—it's always so quiet and peaceful. Never any disturbances. Just the sweet, friendly sounds of nature ... (*We hear gunshots*). Oh, no! Not again! That can only mean one thing! The Hatfields and the McCoys are feuding again!

(*Pa Hatfield enters.*)

HATFIELD: Halt! Who goes there! Friend or foe?

DAISY: It's just me! Daisy Kook!

HATFIELD: Oh. Howdy, Daisy.

DAISY: Don't you "howdy" me! Just what do you think you're doing, Pa Hatfield?

HATFIELD: I'm out hunting McCoys! It's open season on those mangy critters!

(*Pa McCoy enters.*)

MCCOY: Who you calling a mangy critter?

HATFIELD: It's a McCoy!

MCCOY: That's right, Hatfield!

HATFIELD: Now we can have it out! Stand aside, Daisy!

DAISY: Now you two just wait a minute! Why are you always feuding, fighting, and fussing?

HATFIELD: Because Gizzard County ain't big enough for the McCoys and Hatfields both! So we want the McCoys and all their kinfolks out!

DAISY: Hatfield, Gizzard County is plenty big enough for everybody!

MCCOY: Daisy, you just don't understand.

DAISY: That's right, McCoy, I *don't* understand! Just why do you hate the Hatfields so much?

MCCOY: Because they're Hatfields! That's reason enough!

DAISY: No it's not!

HATFIELD: Our families have always fought! It's a tradition!

MCCOY: That's right. And the Bible says "an eye for an eye, and tooth for a tooth"!

DAISY: Now you listen here, you 'ole rascals. Settling problems by fighting went out with the Old Testament. Jesus said we're supposed to love our enemies, and pray for those who hate us.

HATFIELD: No way, Daisy!

DAISY: You know what the trouble with you two is? You're both prejudiced.

MCCOY: What?

DAISY: That's right! Your families hate each other for no reason. Just like some folks are prejudiced against black people, oriental people, or some other race of people.

HATFIELD: Now wait a minute, Daisy—

DAISY: It's true and you know it! Don't you realize we're all related to one another?

MCCOY: I ain't related to no Hatfields!

DAISY: Yes you are! We all come from a common ancestry. The Bible says so. And God created all people and races equal. God loves everybody equally, and so should we.

HATFIELD: Maybe you're right. I'm willing to call a truce iffin he will.

MCCOY: All right, a cease-fire it is!

DAISY: Now you're talking! But remember, without Jesus living and growing in your hearts and changing your attitudes, you'll never find peace with your brothers, or with yourself.

HATFIELD: Daisy, now that we can't fight, what are we going to do with our time?

MCCOY: I've got an idea! We could appear on that game show, "Family Feud"! We'd be naturals!

HATFIELD: That's a great idea! And my family would win all kinds of prizes, because any Hatfield is smarter than a McCoy!

MCCOY: Why, you got a chicken gizzard for a brain, Hatfield!

DAISY: Now boys, remember the truce!

HATFIELD: She's right. I apologize.

DAISY: That's more like it. What you boys need to do is spend some time reading the Bible and applying it to your lives.

HATFIELD: You're right, Daisy.

MCCOY: Come on, Daisy—and you too, Hatfield—let's go over to my shack. I just put in a new satellite dish and big screen TV. How I can get "Hee Haw" twenty-four hours a day!

DAISY: All right! Let's go!

(*They all exit.*)

44.
The Greatest American Puppet

(*A girl enters.*)

GIRL: Help! Help! Somebody help me! My dog has run away, and I can't find him!

(*A boy wearing a red cape enters.*)

BOY: This looks like a job for the Greatest American Puppet! I'll help you find your dog!

GIRL: *Who* are you? Are you on your way to a costume party?

BOY: Naw! I'm the Greatest American Puppet!

GIRL: I don't believe it.

BOY: But I can fly just like Superman!

GIRL: I don't even believe Superman can fly.

BOY: But I've got all kinds of super powers.

GIRL: I don't believe that, either.

BOY: Do you believe in Wonder Woman?

GIRL: No.

BOY: The Incredible Hulk?

GIRL Nope.

BOY: Santa Claus?

GIRL: Of course not.

BOY: Do you believe in *anybody*?

GIRL: I believe in Jesus.

BOY: What?

GIRL: Look, everybody's saying believe in this, believe in that. It's easy to watch television and movies and get caught up in some fantasy. But there's only one person you should really believe in—and that's Jesus Christ.

BOY: Why should I believe in Him? Has He got superpowers?

GIRL: He can do anything! He's the Son of God. And He wants to be with you all the time—to help and guide you.

BOY: Wow!

GIRL: He's the greatest! He'll open up a whole new world for you. He'll show you the way to Heaven, show you the truth about things, and light up your life!

BOY: How do I get to know Jesus?

GIRL: Hang up your cape, turn off the TV, and pick up your Bible.

(*A dog enters with a booklet in his mouth.*)

DOG: Arf! Arf!

GIRL: Arfy! There you are! Where have you been?

BOY: What's that in his mouth?

GIRL: It's a Sunday-school booklet! So that's where he's been! Good dog!

BOY: What's Sunday school?

GIRL: That's a place where you can learn about Jesus. Attend Sunday school at your local church. Your teacher will help you understand your Bible.

BOY: Okay! I'll go just as soon as I ... change clothes.

GIRL: Well, you'd better hurry up! It's already Sunday morning!

BOY: Don't worry! I'm faster than a speeding baseball! And away I go! Up, up and away! Aiiiyyyye!

(*He falls. We hear crashes.*)

GIRL: I don't believe it ... Come on, Arfy!

DOG: Arf! Arf!

(*The girl and the dog exit.*)

45.
Professor
Marvel's
Magic
Elixir

(*Marvel enters.*)

MARVEL: Hurry! Hurry! Hurry! Step right up for Professor Marvel's Magic Elixir! It's good for what ails you—it never fails you! Step right up!

MAN: Oh, Professor Marvel, can you help me?

MARVEL: What seems to be the trouble, my good fellow?

MAN: Can't you tell? I've got a terrible case of dandruff! Just watch. (*Shakes his head.*)

MARVEL: Suffering succotash! Worst case of dandruff I've ever seen. But I've got just the thing for it. Professor Marvel's Magic Elixir! Just rub it into your hair thirty-seven times a day for six months.

MAN: But that means I'd have to buy a truckload of that stuff!

MARVEL: Right you are! And you'll find it worth every penny! Just step behind the curtain and pay my assistant ... (*Man exits.*) Step right up, folks, for Professor Marvel's Magic Elixir! It's good for frostbite and sunburn, and carries the Goodhousekeeping Seal of Approval!

(*A woman enters, crying.*)

WOMAN: Oh, Professor Marvel, it's terrible! Just terrible!

MARVEL: What seems to be the trouble, my little begonia?

WOMAN: I have a flat tire! And I don't know

how to change it.

MARVEL: What you need is a bottle of my magic elixir, my little, daffodil!

WOMAN: It's good for *flat tires* ?

MARVEL: It's good for everything! Just step behind the curtain for your own personal bottle, my little dandelion!

WOMAN: Oh, thank you!

MARVEL: Think nothing of it, my little chicka-dee! (*Woman exits.*) Step right up! Step right up! this magic elixir has been used by pharaohs and kings! Its secret formula has been passed from generation to generation for thousands of years!

(*Maynard enters,*)

MAYNARD: Can you help me? My name is Maynard—and I'm very depressed.

MARVEL: If my name was Maynard, I'd be depressed too.

MAYNARD: No, no, it's not that. It's my girlfriend—she's run off and joined the circus!

MARVEL: Despicable! Absolutely despicable!

MAYNARD: She left me high and dry to join up with some professor that sells tonic or medicine or something.

MARVEL: She did?! Well, my magic elixir is just the thing you need to lift your spirits, but I don't think you should meet my new assistant—I'm still breaking her in. Why don't you come back later and I'll handle your order personally.

MAYNARD: That's mighty nice of you.

(*Maynard exits.*)

MARVEL: Think nothing of it! Hurry! Hurry! Hurry!

(*A boy with a Bible enters.*)

BOY: What you got there, mister?

MARVEL: The answer to all of your problems—just what you need.

BOY: But I've already got the answer to all of my problems right here.

MARVEL: What have you got there?

BOY: It's my Bible.

MARVEL: So that Bible has all the answers, huh, kid?

BOY: Well, it tells you what to do when you're frightened, lonely, depressed, sick, bankrupt, lost, deserted, defeated, confused, weak....

MARVEL: Suffering succotash!

BOY: And if that's not enough, it points the way to *the* answer.

MARVEL: *The* answer? You mean there *is* one answer for all of life's problems?

BOY: Sure! The answer for everything—is Jesus! And the Bible tells all about Him!

MARVEL: What's the secret formula?

BOY: There's no secret formula! All you have to do is read the Bible and learn about Jesus—and accept Him as your Savior. And He's absolutely free—He's already paid the cost for all of us.

MARVEL: Free! Oh, no! You're going to put me out of business!

BOY: Step right up and learn about Jesus! Hurry, hurry, hurry! Learn to live like Him! Learn to trust Him! He's the *real* answer for all your problems!

MARVEL: Go away kid! I don't need the competition!

BOY: Hurry, hurry, hurry! Read the Bible every day—that'll keep those blues away! Step right up!

MARVEL: I give up! If anybody wants me, I'll be in the unemployment line!

(*Marvel exits.*)

BOY: (*Laughs*) Come one, come all! And learn about Jesus! Hurry! Hurry! Hurry!

(*The boy exits.*)

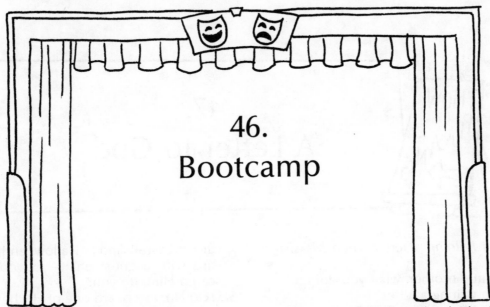

46.
Bootcamp

(*The Sarge and Gilbert enter.*)

SARGE (*screaming*): All right, soldier! Atten hut! (*Gilbert follows Sarge's orders.*) Right face! Left face! About face! Face front! Up face! Down face! All-around face! March! One, two, three, four! Hut! Hut! Hut! At ease! (*Gilbert drops over from exhaustion.*) What's your name, boy?

GILBERT: Gilbert, sir.

SARGE: Well, Gilbert, I'm going to make a soldier out of you!

GILBERT: Yes, sir, sergeant.

SARGE: I can't hear you!

GILBERT (*louder*): Yes, sir, sergeant!

SARGE: So you want to be a soldier, uh boy?

GILBERT: No sir, I want to be a ballet dancer. Ha, ha, ha!

SARGE (*screams*): I don't like your sense of humor, boy!

GILBERT: Sorry, sir!

SARGE: Right now you're a puny Mickey Mouse! But I'm going to make you into a big, mean, green, army machine!

GILBERT: Yes, sir!

SARGE: But first you have to be trained! That's why you're here in bootcamp! Everybody has to go through basic training! You don't become a soldier overnight!

GILBERT: I know that, sergeant! It's the same way in God's army! First you have to believe that Jesus is God's Son, and then you have to be taught how to follow Him.

SARGE: That's right, boy! Say where'd you learn all that?

GILBERT: At (*enter the name of your church*) sir, back home in (*enter the name of your city*).

SARGE: Well, they taught you right, boy.

GILBERT: I've learned a lot of what I know over the years in Sunday school. That's kind of like bootcamp. That's where they teach kids how to follow Jesus into victory!

SARGE: We're going to take that old devil by the nose and kick him in the pants!

GILBERT: We're going to march over him and storm the enemy's gates!

SARGE: We're going to beat him with the Word of God! And we're going to win this war!

GILBERT: That's right, sergeant!

SARGE: But first, we have to be trained! We have to learn how to live, how to win, and how to follow Jesus!

GILBERT: Yes, sir!

SARGE: I'm signing up for Sunday school! And you're coming with me!

GILBERT: Yes, sir!

SARGE: Atten hut! About face, right face, left face, up face, down face! Quit poking around, boy! March! One, two, three, four! Hut, hut, hut!

(*They exit.*)

47.
A Letter to God

(*A boy enters holding a letter. Then his sister enters.*)

SISTER: Hey, little brother, what you doing?

BROTHER: I'm writing a letter.

SISTER: I'll bet I know who it's to!

BROTHER: I'll bet you don't!

SISTER: I'll bet I do!

BROTHER: I'll bet you don't

SISTER: It's to Santa Claus!

BROTHER: Nope!

SISTER: The Easter Bunny?

BROTHER: Nope!

SISTER: A movie star?

BROTHER: Nope!

SISTER: Your girlfriend?

BROTHER (*shaking his head*): Naw . . .

SISTER: Then who are you writing to?

BROTHER: I'm writing to God!

SISTER: Ha! Ha! Boy, are you dumb! I suppose you're going to mail it to Heaven! Ha! Ha! Ha!

BROTHER: I don't have to mail it!

SISTER: Then how's He going to get it, smarty, if you don't mail it to Him?

BROTHER: Don't call me "smarty"! I don't have to mail it to Him because God sees *everything*! So if I write God a letter, He's going to see it and He's going to read it!

SISTER (*surprised*): Yeah?

BROTHER: Yeah! *You* could write a letter to God! Anybody could! And God will read it! I'm going to take *my* letter and put it in my Bible.

SISTER: And God will *really* read it?

BROTHER: He reads all His mail! Just like He listens to every prayer!

SISTER: Wow. . . .

BROTHER: You know something else?

SISTER: What?

BROTHER: God *likes* to get letters! And He likes to hear prayers! He just likes to hear from us all the time—He's really nice. At Christmas, I sent Him a birthday card! I sent Him a valentine on Valentine's Day! I sent Him an Easter card at Easter! And at Halloween I sent Him a card with a ghost on it—you don't think it scared Him, do you?

SISTER: No. I've heard one of His best friends is the Holy Ghost.

BROTHER: Anyway, I write to God every chance I get. And talk to Him every night!

SISTER: I think I'll write a letter to God, too! (*The brother and sister exit.*)

48. David and Goliath

(Howard enters.)

HOWARD: Good afternon, ladies and gentlemen. This is Howard Cordial coming to you live from the land of Judah in the Middle East. We are here today to present the championship bout between David of Israel and Goliath of Gath. And an interesting fight it promises to be. On one side we have a giant Philistine, and on the other, a lowly shepherd boy, plucked from obscurity, and thrust suddenly into the limelight as he challenges a champion. Let us go now into the Philistine camp for a few words from Goliath—a towering figure of a man rising nearly nine feet tall.

(Goliath enters.)

HOWARD: Goliath, just what are we going to see out here today?

GOLIATH: Well, Howard, as you know, I am the greatest! I'm gonna float like a butterfly, sting like a bee! I'm gonna grab him and not let him go! I'm going to hit him high, and I'm going to hit him low! And that's not all I'm going to do! When I'm done, he will be through!

HOWARD: Thank you, Goliath. (Goliath exits.) We now take you to the Israeli camp for a few words from David—an unassuming young man quite small in stature in comparison with Goliath. And here he comes now!

(*David enters.*)

HOWARD: David, if we could have a moment of your time. . . .

DAVID: Certainly, Howard.

HOWARD: David, this giant has threatened you with great harm.

DAVID: That's right, Howard.

HOWARD: He has even threatened you with fatal injury.

DAVID: That's right, Howard.

HOWARD: Do you have any reply to these threats?

DAVID: I only have one thing to say to Goliath, Howard—he's finished!

HOWARD: David, I understand you're a shepherd, and a musician of some repute.

DAVID: Yes, Howard.

HOWARD: What makes you think you can stand up against this professional soldier, this giant Philistine, this—if I may say—subhuman barbarian? What makes you think you can stand up against such a man?

DAVID: Howard, I'm not going out there to fight him alone. I'm going out there with the Lord of hosts, with the God of the armies of Israel! I feel sorry for the man, Howard, I really do—he doesn't have a chance! You see, it's not really me he's up against—he's up against the power of God!

HOWARD: David, you're just a kid—how can you say you have the power of God in your life?

DAVID: Because there's power in the Word of God! And I have the Word in my heart, and the Holy Spirit in my life! That's an unbeatable combination! For example, it is written, "The battle is the Lord's." So I know that if God wants this man dead, He will deliver Goliath into my hands.

HOWARD: Well, you're certainly an inspiration to us all.

DAVID: If you'll excuse me now, Howard, I have to go pick up some stones for my slingshot.

HOWARD: Certainly . . . (*David exits.*) Ladies and gentlemen, I'm now standing overlooking the battlefield, the Valley of Elah. There's a feeling of tenseness in the air. Both camps are watching closely as the two challengers approach each other on the field below. . . . David has broken into a run, and is heading toward Goliath, the sling already whirling over his head! Goliath has also stepped up his pace. His spear is raised—and a big spear it is, ladies and gentlemen—and he's ready to throw it. But wait! David has let fly his first stone! And Goliath is hit! And he's down! Ladies and gentlemen, Goliath is down! David has now reached the fallen giant—it's all over for Goliath, folks You should hear the cheers going up in the Israeli camp! And as for the Philistines, they seem to have taken flight! The Israelis are now taking off in hot pursuit, obviously seeing a chance to turn the tables on their enemies! Well, there you have it, ladies and gentlemen, quite an exciting afternoon. And as for the new champ, David of Israel, I think we'll be hearing more about this young man in the future ... This is Howard Cordial signing off!

(*Howard exits.*)

49.
A Christmas Without Santa

(*An immobile snowman, made from Styrofoam balls, and Shirley Demples are on stage. Shirley is finishing the snowman.*)

SHIRLEY: Just a little more snow right here ought to do it. There! The perfect snowman!

MOM'S VOICE (*from offstage*): Shirley! Time to come in now! Bedtime!

SHIRLEY: Coming mother! (*To herself*): But I'm too excited to sleep! It's too close to Christmas! I wonder what I'm going to get this year? I sure wish I could peek inside Santa's workshop right about now.

SNOWMAN: If you did, you would be disappointed.

SHIRLEY: Yipes! Who said that?

SNOWMAN: I did.

SHIRLEY: A talking snowman?

SNOWMAN: Why not? Is it not written in the Bible that the heavens *declare* the glory of God? Why, a few days ago, I was just moisture in the sky hovering over the North Pole. Then I rode down a polar air mass and fell in this part of the world.

SHIRLEY: That's incredible.

SNOWMAN: Then you gathered me up and made me into a snowman.

SHIRLEY: So you know what's going on in Santa's workshop?

SNOWMAN: I'm afraid Santa's workshop is idle. The lights have been dimmed. And sound of deep sighing has replaced the usual joy and laughter.

SHIRLEY: Why is that?

SNOWMAN: For the first time since his creation, Santa is very sad. And nobody knows why.

SHIRLEY: If I could go to the North Pole, I'd cheer him up!

SNOWMAN: What's stopping you?

SHIRLEY: How would I get there?

SNOWMAN: Use your imagination! It's a very powerful tool! If you can believe in talking snowmen, then a trip to the North Pole should be no trouble at all. Tonight, as you sleep, dream a dream about it. Who knows what might happen?

SHIRLEY: All right, I'll try it. Goodnight, Mr. Snowman.

SNOWMAN: Pleasant dreams.

(*Shirley and the snowman exit. We hear the sound of Christmas bells. And after a pause, Santa enters. The bells fade out.*)

SANTA: Woe is me! Woe is me! No one understands! Woe is me.

(*Shirley enters.*)

SHIRLEY: I don't believe it! I'm here—I'm really here!

SANTA: Do my eyes deceive me? Aren't you Shirley Demples?

SHIRLEY: That's right, Santa.

SANTA: How did you get up here to the North Pole?

SHIRLEY: I was dreaming … I was swimming in the Gulf of Mexico when suddenly this hurricane came up! I was pulled up the funnel into the upper atmosphere. And there I rode a tropical air mass all the way to the North Pole where I was dropped with a lot of snow!

SANTA: Such an imagination! I suppose you've come to take a peek into my workshop like the kid last week. He had a much smoother ride up here. He dreamed he was on the starship Enterprise and Scotty beamed him down.

SHIRLEY: No, Santa. I heard you've been sad, so I've come to cheer you up.

SANTA: Then you've wasted a good dream. I'm beyond cheering up. Santa Claus is finished! I'm through with this job! I quit!

SHIRLEY: What's the matter?

SANTA: No one understands me anymore. It has gotten worse each year.

SHIRLEY: Would you like to talk about it? Maybe I can help.

SANTA: Don't you see, little one? The world has exploited me—manipulated me! Changed me into something I was never meant to be.

SHIRLEY: What do you mean?

SANTA: Once, a long time ago, I was called St. Nicholas. I was named after a bishop who had a reputation for kindness and charity—especially toward children. He pointed the way to

Jesus through his life and teachings. So great was his influence, that a holiday was created to remember him. And the tradition of exchanging gifts was born.

SHIRLEY: Then what happened?

SANTA: Well, a little while after that, I became known in other parts of the world as Kriss Kringle—which means "Christ Child." Many people used to believe that the baby Jesus would manifest Himself every Christmas by leaving gifts for children. In part, they were right. Jesus was God's great gift—a living sacrifice for the world. But over the years they turned Kriss Kringle into an old man with a magical flying sleigh ... (*sighs*). Sometimes an imagination can be a bad thing—especially when fanciful notions hide the truth.

SHIRLEY: But now you're called Santa Claus. What does that mean?

SANTA: It's merely an Americanized version of the old Dutch form of St. Nicholas—Sinterklaas, I believe.

SHIRLEY: Do you have any other names?

SANTA: Oh, yes! I have more names than my eight reindeer. Everything from Father Christmas to Grandfather Frost. Sometimes I have a hard time remembering who I am myself! And with the name changes came confusion over what I represented. People began forgetting what I stood for. They started commercializing me! The world has turned me into an idol! They've put me in parades, in stores, in books, on television. Greedy merchants have me promoting everything from Rambo dolls to Japanese sportscars!

SHIRLEY: Not all merchants are greedy, Santa!

SANTA: You're right. I'm sorry. I get carried away. Forgive me. I just get so upset when I see what's happening. Why, just look at what gift giving has turned into. It all started when the Wise-men brought gifts to the baby Jesus. But now it's turned into traffic jams, Christmas sales, tired feet, and shattered nerves. People give more out of obligation than love. And more often than not, they forget about the poor!

SHIRLEY: What about the joyous voices of carolers ringing out across the world? Doesn't that lift your Christmas spirit?

SANTA: Have you listened to what they're singing? Christmas hymns have been replaced by Christmas disco, Christmas rock, and Christmas fever. They're all singing about Rudolph, Frosty the Snowman, Jack Frost, and, of course, Santa. Woe is me! They're using *me* to take people's eyes off what Christmas is really all about.

SHIRLEY: What *is* Christmas all about?

(*Gentle theme music begins*)

SANTA: Almost two thousand years ago, a new hope was born to the world in the form of a man-child. The child was a new beginning for us all. He was the Savior, Jesus Christ. It's His entrance into the world we are supposed to be celebrating with great joy and reverence. Without Jesus in the human heart, Christmas goodwill melts away like the snow.

SHIRLEY: Santa, if that's true, then *you* can have a new beginning.

SANTA: What?

SHIRLEY: You can start over and declare a *new* message! And become a *new* symbol. No more "Merry Christmas! Ho, ho, ho!" but "Joy to the world, the Lord is come!"

SANTA (*begins to get excited*): It will be a new Christmas!.... I'll begin today! Throw away the past! And the Christmas I'll help make this year will last! Because I'll be declaring the eternal message of God's love and forgiveness through His Son!

SHIRLEY: Now you're talking, Santa!

SANTA: Oh, my, look at the time! I've got to get going! I've got to be in a parade in New York! But first I think I'll stop by a Christian bookstore.

SHIRLEY: Why?

SANTA: I want to pick up a Jesus bumper sticker for my sleigh! Want to ride along?

SHIRLEY: Sure! But you'll have to hurry! I'll be waking up soon!

SANTA (*laughs*): Ho, ho, ho, ho, ho, ho, ho ...

(*Santa and Shirley exit.*)

50.
Lazarus

(*Lazarus and his friend enter from opposite directions.*)

FRIEND: Hey, Lazarus, old buddy! It's good to see you!

LAZARUS: And it's good to see you, my old friend! How have you been?

FRIEND: Oh, fine, fine. Can't complain. But I hear *you've* been sick.

LAZARUS: That's right. I was *very* sick.

FRIEND: What did you have? A touch of the Roman flu or something?

LAZARUS: No.

FRIEND: Maybe a little hay fever? It's that time of year.

LAZARUS: No, no I had a very serious disease. What you might call a *fatal* disease.

FRIEND: Wow! It's a miracle you survived.

LAZARUS: I didn't survive . . . I died.

FRIEND: You *what*?

LAZARUS: I died. I was sick for a few days, and then I kicked the bucket!

FRIEND: Oh, I see! You mean your heart stopped beating, and then they brought you back to life right away with a little artificial resuscitation. Is that it?

LAZARUS: No! I was dead for four days.

FRIEND: Four days?!

LAZARUS: That's right.

FRIEND: Oh, come on!

LAZARUS: It's true. They wrapped me up like a mummy and even buried me!

FRIEND: Then that can mean only one thing! You're a ghost! Aiiiiiii!

LAZARUS: No, no! I'm not a ghost! I'm just as much alive as you are!

FRIEND: Well then, how were you brought back to life?

LAZARUS: I was brought back to life by a good friend of mine—Jesus of Nazareth.

FRIEND: I've heard of Him! He calls himself the Messiah! The Son of the living God!

LAZARUS: He is! And I'm *living* proof of it!

FRIEND: Amazing! Tell me, why do you think you were brought back?

LAZARUS: Probably so our Lord Jesus could display His mighty power—power over even life and death. And I suppose so I could be a witness to what's on the "other side."

FRIEND: Yes! What *is* on the other side? Where did you go after you died?

LAZARUS: I went to Heaven, of course!

FRIEND: You've seen Heaven?

LAZARUS: Yes, indeed! I was escorted there by an angel!

FRIEND: An angel! What was the angel like?

LAZARUS: He was huge! And powerful! And very friendly toward me. He told me he had been my guardian angel all my life!

FRIEND: Incredible!

LAZARUS: I even feel like he's watching over me now—like a big brother who is always with me!

FRIEND: What was Heaven like?

LAZARUS: It was beautiful! More beautiful than Bethlehem in the spring. Trees, flowers, grass—it must have been what the garden of Eden was like! And then there was the heavenly city called New Jerusalem! Oh, my friend, if only I could describe it! Shining streets of gold! Gates of pearl! Walls of precious stones! People singing for joy! Such happiness! Such peacefulness! There's no sorrow or tears up there! I almost wish I hadn't come back.

FRIEND: Lazarus, old buddy, I want to meet this friend of yours! This Jesus!

LAZARUS: Well, come on! I'll introduce you to Him!

FRIEND: All right! Let's go! But first I want to apologize.

LAZARUS: Apologize for what?

FRIEND: For not going to your funeral—I didn't hear about it in time.

LAZARUS (*laughs*): That's all right! You can go to my next one!

(*They both laugh and exit.*)

51. Casting Your Cares

(Jeffries and Buford the mule enter.)

JEFFRIES: Sir Nigel Jeffries here, world famous explorer, with another edition of everyone's favorite animal program, Mutual of Okinawa's Wild Manimal Kingdom; the show that brings you animals caught in the act of being themselves—sort of the animal world's version of "Candid Camera." Ha! Ha! Yes, I've been from Borneo to Zamboanga looking for the strange, the unusual, the bizarre!

BUFORD: Why didn't you just look in the mirror? Yuk! Yuk!

JEFFRIES (Clears throat): Yes, well ... Our guest today is that very common beast of burden, the donkey. (Addresses Buford): Tell us, are you a wild donkey?

BUFORD: Only on Saturday nights!

JEFFRIES: I see. Is it true that donkeys are stubborn?

BUFORD: No more than a lot of people I know!

JEFFRIES (laughs): Jolly good! Tell us, what are some things you do as a beast of burden?

BUFORD: I mostly carry heavy loads.

JEFFRIES: Doesn't that get rather tiring?

BUFORD: Not usually. Donkeys have strong legs and a strong back. But even so, there are some things I absolutely refuse to carry!

JEFFRIES: Like what?

BUFORD: I refuse to carry disappointments and failures—they're really heavy.

JEFFRIES: Disappointments and failures?

BUFORD: That's right. And I refuse to drag around the past all the time. I forget those things that are in the past and I live for today and the future.

JEFFRIES: I see, how very interesting.

BUFORD: I also refuse to carry heartaches—they'll weigh you down real fast. And I won't carry around worries, fears, and anxieties either. There isn't a saddle bag big enough to hold all those anyway.

JEFFRIES: Is there anything else you refuse to carry?

BUFORD: Yep. I refuse to carry unforgiveness, jealousy, anger, and sin. None of those will ever be a passenger on my back.

JEFFRIES: But what do you do when they try to climb on?

BUFORD: I just shake them off! Shake them off! Remember the Bible story about Apostle Paul? He was collecting firewood when a snake bit him and fastened onto his hand. Well, he didn't panic or worry about it, he just shook that ole snake off. And that's what I do with my worries and cares.

JEFFRIES: But someone has to deal with all those burdens, old chap. They don't just go away, you know. They need to be carried out of our life.

BUFORD: That's right. And I let the Lord do the carrying. He carries all my burdens—if I let Him. It says in the Bible, "Cast all your cares on the Lord, because He careth for you." Why not take advantage of that?

JEFFRIES: But don't you carry anything?

BUFORD: I like to carry a smile on my face, a song on my lips, and the love of Jesus in my heart. Those are light things—but they're worth a lot.

JEFFRIES: I see what you mean.

BUFORD: And also, whenever I can, I try to help carry someone else's load—because when burdens are shared, they're lighter for everyone! Besides, the more you help someone else, the more help you'll receive in a time of need.

JEFFRIES: What else do donkeys do?

BUFORD: Donkeys are good at climbing mountains, because we're very sure-footed.

JEFFRIES: I wish I could climb some mountains—some spiritual mountains, that is. I always seem to be in the valleys of life.

BUFORD: All you need to be sure-footed yourself is to follow in the footsteps of Jesus. And He'll lead you through those valleys and you'll soon be climbing the mountains of God!

JEFFRIES: I say, this conversation has been very enlightening.

BUFORD: Donkeys are good at giving advice. Why, in the Bible, if Balaam the prophet had paid attention to his talking donkey, he would have saved himself a lot of trouble.

JEFFRIES: And if God can talk through a donkey, then He can talk through anybody who is willing to speak up for Him.

BUFORD: That's right!

JEFFRIES: And so, ladies and gentlemen, on that positive note, this is Sir Nigel Jeffries and Buford T. Mule saying, cheerio everybody!

(Jeffries and Buford exit.)

54. The Watchdog

(Jeffries enters.)

JEFFRIES: Sir Nigel Jeffries here with everyone's favorite animal program—Mutual of Okinawa Wild Manimal Kingdom. The show that brings you lions and tigers and bears—oh my! We bring you *all* kinds of animals—occasionally even heavy metal rock singers! Ha! Ha! We always have our tranquilizer guns ready when they're around—you never know what they'll do! But today we have a tamer species of animal, the canine—otherwise known as man's best friend, the dog! (Hugo the dog enters barking.) Down, Rover! Down, boy!

HUGO: My name is Hugo—not Rover. Hugo Humongus.

JEFFRIES: Sorry about that, old boy.

HUGO: It doesn't matter. A dog by *any* name would still lick your face. We're a very lovable species. I wish I could say the same about people.

JEFFRIES: And just what kind of a dog are you?

HUGO: I'm a *big* dog.

JEFFRIES: Do you have a pedigree.

HUGO: A WHAT?

JEFFRIES: Do you have a pedigree?

HUGO: No—I didn't go to college.

JEFFRIES: No, no! A pedigree is a list of your ancestors showing that you're pure bred in your bloodline.

HUGO: The only way any of us can ever really be pure is to allow Jesus to cleanse us with His blood.

JEFFRIES: I see....

HUGO: I also happen to be a watchdog.

JEFFRIES: A watchdog, eh? Well tell me, what time is it?

HUGO: I don't know. How would I know what time it is?

JEFFRIES: Well, if you're a *watch* dog, you should know what time it is! Ha! Ha! A little reporter humor there! Ha! Ha!

HUGO: I'll tell you what time it is! It's later than you think!

JEFFRIES: What do you mean?

HUGO: You know, some people watch celebrities, some people watch television, some watch movies, some watch sports, and that's *all* they watch. You know what I watch? I watch for the second coming of Jesus! Which is just around the corner. So, I'm keeping my eyes wide open and my heart tuned to God.

JEFFRIES: Tell me, Hugo, why is it that dogs like to bury bones?

HUGO: Well, where else are we going to put them? Have you ever seen a dog with a refrigerator in his doghouse?

JEFFRIES: I never thought of that.

HUGO: Besides, whenever I bury a bone, I pretend I'm burying my past sins and mistakes—and I don't dig them up again! People should do that. God forgives and forgets, and so should we.

JEFFRIES: Hugo, is it true that dogs don't like cats?

HUGO: I *love* cats.

JEFFRIES: You *do?*

HUGO: Sure! Especially with lots of ketchup and mustard! (*Barks and pants.*)

JEFFRIES: And is it true that dogs are really man's best friend?

HUGO: Not by a long shot! Sure, we're loyal, true-blue, good natured, loving, and fun; but the best friend man ever had was Jesus, because God so loved the world, that He gave His only begotten Son, so that whosoever would believe in Him wouldn't perish in their sins, but would have everlasting life instead. He came to give men a second chance, a brand new life, and to help men where they couldn't help themselves.

JEFFRIES: I must say, you're certainly a frisky canine. Do I detect what they call the Hi Pro glow?

HUGO: Naw—that's just the Holy Spirit! The Holy Spirit will give you a glow! And it will make you frisky too!

JEFFRIES: One last question. Do you do any tricks?

HUGO: Do I do tricks?! Of course! Just a second! (*He exits and returns with a mouthful of cards.*) Pick a card, any card! But don't let me see it!

JEFFRIES: I don't mean card tricks!

HUGO (*spits out cards*): I'm also pretty good at pulling a rabbit out of a hat.

JEFFRIES: But can you roll over, fetch, and beg?

HUGO: Anybody can do that! *You* could do that. Right now I'm working on a disappearing act. I'm trying to make my fleas disappear—they're driving me crazy!

JEFFRIES: I think it's time we *both* disappeared. This is Sir Nigel Jeffries and Hugo saying, cheerio everybody! (*Hugo barks.*)

(*Jeffries and Hugo exit.*)

55.
The Chicken

JEFFRIES: Sir Nigel Jeffries here once again with everybody's favorite animal program—you guessed it!—Mutual of Okinawa's Wild Manimal Kingdom. I've been around the world and under the sea to bring you glimpses of our little animal friends. I've done everything from brushing the teeth of a shark to petting a porcupine! But today we have a departure from the exotic. We have a report on a common ordinary, everyday, run-of-the-mill barnyard chicken.

CHICKEN (*clucking as she enters*): Just who are you calling ordinary? I'll have you know I only lay grade double-A eggs!

JEFFRIES: Sorry about that, old girl! I didn't mean to ruffle your feathers!

CHICKEN: You've got a lot of nerve!

JEFFRIES: Why, you're as angry as a wet hen, if you'll pardon the pun! Ha! Ha!

CHICKEN: How would you like it if I called you a common, ordinary, run-of-the-mill explorer?

JEFFRIES: Why, I'm famous the world over! Especially in the jungle! One morning I even shot a lion in my pajamas! How he got in my pajamas I'll never know....

CHICKEN: Then you see what I mean?!

JEFFRIES: Yes, you've made your point.

CHICKEN: All of God's creatures, even humans, are special and unique. There's not another you, and there's not another me. And God loves each of us as individuals.

JEFFRIES: You're absolutely right.

CHICKEN: And what's more, God has a wonderful, special plan for my life that only I can do. And He has a plan just for you, too.

JEFFRIES: Really?

CHICKEN: Absolutely! And if you follow God's plan, you'll have an abundant and happy life. But if you go your own way in life, you better watch out! There's no telling what will happen!

JEFFRIES: How very interesting.

CHICKEN: Say, you're not related to Colonel Sanders are you?

JEFFRIES: Of course not.

CHICKEN: What about Ronald McDonald?

JEFFRIES: No.

CHICKEN: Thank goodness!

JEFFRIES: What's wrong with Ronald McDonald?

CHICKEN: Haven't you ever heard of Chicken McNuggets?

JEFFRIES: Oh, yes, I forgot. Rest assured, I'm only here to ask you a few questions to enlighten our audience about chickens.

CHICKEN: Questions like what?

JEFFRIES: For example, is it true that chickens can't fly?

CHICKEN: What do you mean? I fly all the time. Sometimes a thousand miles in one day!

JEFFRIES: Really? That's incredible! How do you do it?

CHICKEN: Mostly through Eastern airlines. They

have great vacations to Florida. But sometimes I go TWA.

JEFFRIES: What I meant was, is it true that chickens can't fly with their own wings?

CHICKEN: You don't need wings to fly! One of these days we're *all* going to fly away—when Jesus comes back and calls us up to meet Him in the air.

JEFFRIES: What about the rumor that all chickens are cowards?

CHICKEN: What? Are you calling us chickens, chicken? Let me tell you, some of the biggest chickens I know are people! But it doesn't have to be that way.

JEFFRIES: What do you mean?

CHICKEN: The Bible says that God doesn't give us a spirit of fear, but of power, and of love, and of a sound mind. It also says that the righteous are as bold as a lion!

JEFFRIES: So some chickens are lions?

CHICKEN: The righteous ones are! Or they should be!

JEFFRIES: Perhaps you could answer this age old question: why did the chicken cross the road?

CHICKEN: He crossed the road to go to church, of course. Some people cross the road to go to bars. Others to ball games. Others go fishing. People are always running here, there, and everywhere. But the one place they really need to be is in God's house. They don't realize that when you put God first, all the other areas of your life will be enriched!

JEFFRIES: And so we come to the end of our barnyard conversation with that most extraordinary and noble animal, the chicken.

CHICKEN: That's more like it!

JEFFRIES: This is Sir Nigel Jeffries and friend saying, be seeing you! Cheerio! Goodbye! Farewell! Adios! And all that other good stuff! (*Jeffries and the chicken exit.*)

98

56.
The Rock Singer

(Jeffries enters.)

JEFFRIES: Ladies and gentlemen, it's time for a very special edition of that amazing animal adventure series, Mutual of Okinawa's Wild Manimal Kingdom. I'm about to profile the most fearsome and ferocious beast I have ever come across. The very thought of standing next to it sends chills down my spine. But the show must go on. I'll do my best to keep this wild animal under control. Here it comes now ... (Mongo enters). Hello there, and what is your name?

MONGO: My name is Mongo.

JEFFRIES: And what kind of an animal are you?

MONGO: I'm a heavy metal rock singer, man.

JEFFRIES: Now, you're not going to bite me, are you?

MONGO: Don't worry, I've had my shots.

JEFFRIES: Just what kind of music do you play?

MONGO: Loud music.

JEFFRIES: And what group do you play with?

MONGO: We call ourselves the Twisted Dead Heads.

JEFFRIES: Just standing next to you makes me nervous.

MONGO: Don't worry, man, I only get violent on stage. But don't provoke me!

JEFFRIES: I wouldn't dream of it, old boy! But I thought they kept you fellows in cages, or at least on a leash.

MONGO: I do have a spiked collar at home I like to wear. But guys like me are free to roam. We like to get into homes with our music, and get into minds. Know what I mean?

JEFFRIES: I'm afraid I do. And what is your inspiration?

MONGO: Money. I love money. And I'll say and do practically anything to get it. I figure I'll only stay on top for a few years—that's the way it is with most rock singers—so I've got to make a killing while I can.

JEFFRIES: I've heard that rock singers tend to have short life spans.

MONGO: That's the breaks, man. One of the hazards of my profession.

JEFFRIES: Of all the animals I've ever interviewed, I think I fear you the most.

MONGO: Why is that?

JEFFRIES: Music is a great means of communication. It can uplift and inspire, or it can depress and destroy. It can lead you to life, or it can lead you to death. It can bring health, or it can be poison. You have a poisonous bite, Mongo, and the young people who play with you often don't realize that.

MONGO: That's heavy, man, but it's not my problem. I'm an animal, remember? I am what I am. I live for myself and feed off the public. They consume my music, and I consume them. Seems fair to me.

JEFFRIES: What are your lyrics about?

MONGO: Some of them are about immoral sex, some are about violence. A lot of my lyrics contain messages that most parents wouldn't be too happy to hear.

JEFFRIES: Why do people listen to stuff like that?

MONGO: People listen to my music because they're looking for answers. They want to know how to live, how to get some satisfaction out of life, how to escape. So I tell them how to do it. I tell them to party and get high.

JEFFRIES: And when they crash?

MONGO: That's not my problem.

JEFFRIES: There's pleasure in sin for a little while, but it eventually leads to death and a destroyed life.

MONGO: Yeah, well, I say live it up and have a good time. And let tomorrow worry about itself.

JEFFRIES: What was your biggest hit, Mongo?

MONGO: It was a song called, "Black is white, night is day, right is wrong, and wrong is right." Sold three million copies.

JEFFRIES: What a gruesome message!

MONGO: You know what kids like about me and my kind? We're bold and aggressive. You want some advice? The church is never going to get anywhere until it becomes bold and aggressive too!

JEFFRIES: I believe you're right. The church, instead of being a domesticated pussycat sitting in a padded pew, needs to become a roaring lion again!

MONGO: Yeah, well, you give the people your message, and I'll give them mine. And we'll see who wins.

JEFFRIES: I already know who's going to win.

MONGO: Well, man, it's time for me to go—it's feeding time! (*Roars.*)

JEFFRIES: And so we come to the end of our interview with this dangerous creature. This is Sir Nigel Jeffries saying, cheerio everybody. That was a close one!

(*Mongo roars again and they both exit.*)

57.
The Turkey

(Jeffries and the turkey enter.)

JEFFRIES: Sir Nigel Jeffries here once again with another edition of everyone's favorite animal program—Mutual of Okinawa's Wild Manimal Kingdom. The program that brings you action, danger, excitement, adventure, thrills, chills, spills. What you might call the animal world's version of the A-Team! Ha! Ha! A little zoological humor there! *(The turkey gobbles.)* Ah, yes, today's specimen is that most interesting of birds, the domestic turkey.

TURKEY: Hey! Who are you calling a specimen! How'd you like to be called a "specimen"? I'll tell you, I get no respect, no respect at all.

JEFFRIES: Sorry about that, old boy. I didn't mean to ruffle your feathers! Ha! Ha!

TURKEY: The name is T, *Mr. T* for Turkey, you know what I mean?

JEFFRIES: You call yourself Mr. T?

TURKEY: That's right. And I'm going to start wearing gold chains, too. Maybe then I'll get a little respect!

JEFFRIES: But don't you think gold chains would look a little silly on a turkey?

TURKEY: Hey, watch who you're calling a turkey, turkey!

JEFFRIES: But you *are* a turkey.

TURKEY: I know that. Just watch how you say it!

JEFFRIES: You seem to be very touchy, I must say.

TURKEY: That's because I get no respect. Everywhere I go—no respect at all. You know what I mean? The other day I walked into McDonald's. They took one look at me and said, "You don't deserve a break today!"

JEFFRIES: That's pretty bad.

TURKEY: Let me tell you, that's not the half of it. One day I went over to the zoo and said, "Hey, I wanna be one of your animals here." They said, "We only take *exotic* animals." I said, "Hey, I was born in Hawaii—how exotic can you get?" And they said, "Get outta here before we feed you to the boa constrictor." I'll tell ya, no respect at all.

JEFFRIES: Ah, but I'll bet you're respected around Thanksgiving time—when the turkey becomes everyone's favorite bird.

TURKEY: Are you kidding? I get rejected for Thanksgiving dinner every year! People take one look at me and go out and buy hamburgers! How degrading! They say I wouldn't even make a decent gravey. Can I help it if I suffer from substandard giblets?

JEFFRIES: You know, it's been said that turkeys aren't very intelligent. Is that true?

TURKEY: You see there—now you're doing it. No respect at all! Just because I think two plus two equals five doesn't mean I'm stupid—just under-educated! But hey, what can I do about it? They don't allow turkeys in grade school. So I'm kind of stuck with just what I know, you know what I mean?

JEFFRIES: I'd say you have a real problem.

TURKEY: You can say that again! If I could just get some respect!

JEFFRIES: Everyone deserves respect. We are all God's creations, after all.

TURKEY: Now you're talking!

JEFFRIES: We shouldn't look down on anyone just because he or she doesn't measure up to our standards.

TURKEY: That's right!

JEFFRIES: Or just because he or she might be a little shy, or a little awkward. Or maybe they're not dressed just right.

TURKEY: I like what you're saying! Keep going!

JEFFRIES: We should especially respect our parents, our teachers, and the elderly.

TURKEY: Hey, right on!

JEFFRIES: And we should respect other's property, too. How would you like it if someone tore up something *you* owned? Do unto others as you would have them do unto you.

TURKEY: Hey, I respect what you're saying there, for sure!

JEFFRIES: And so, on that note of mutual respect and admiration, this is Sir Nigel Jeffries and Mr. T saying cheerio! *(The turkey gobbles.)*

(Jeffries and the turkey exit.)

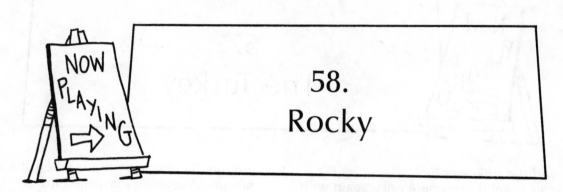

58.
Rocky

(*Howard enters.*)

HOWARD: Good afternoon, ladies and gentlemen. This is Howard Cordial coming to you live from Philadelphia where we will soon have an interview with that fearless fighter, Rocky Bamboa, as he prepares for yet another fight—the greatest fight of his life. And here he comes now! (*Rocky enters.*) Rocky, could we have a moment of your time?

ROCKY: I suppose I could break training for a moment, Howard.

HOWARD: I understand you're about to face the greatest challenge of your life.

ROCKY: That's right, Howard. This is the big one. And I'm going all the way!

HOWARD: But who are you going to fight? Who is your challenger?

ROCKY: I'm going up against the devil, Howard. And I'm going to beat him!

HOWARD: The devil? But, Rocky, who's your trainer? Who can train you to fight the devil?

ROCKY: The Holy Spirit is my trainer, Howard. And the Bible is my training manual.

HOWARD: And just where is this fight going to take place?

ROCKY: In a special arena, Howard—the arena of life. In my life, your life, everybody's life. We all have to face the devil. But I'm going up against him with the Lord on my side—so I know I'm going to win!

HOWARD: Well, good luck, Rocky.

ROCKY: Thank you, Howard. (*Howard exits.*) Now to get back to my training!

(*A black man, Mr. B, enters wearing gold chains.*)

MR. B: Hey, Rocky! Rocky Bamboa! I mean you!

ROCKY: Hey, Mr. B, how you doing, man?

MR. B: I heard you gotta fight coming up.

ROCKY: That's right, man.

MR. B: Well, I've come to help you out. I'm gonna put you on the Mr. B workout. Every morning your gonna get up at 4:00 a.m., eat four raw eggs, and then go out jogging for fifteen miles. Then you're gonna come back and punch out a side of beef! You follow that and you'll soon be a lean, mean, fighting machine. And your opponent will be dog meat!

ROCKY: I'd rather be strong in the Lord and let Him fight my battles.

MR. B: Listen to me, Rocky. There's one solution to every problem—force and violence! Whosoever has the biggest weapon and the strongest fist wins.

ROCKY: Just like Goliath, eh?

MR. B: What you talking about, Rocky?

ROCKY: You remember the story of David and Goliath? David was just a little kid—and he beat a giant because David was strong in the Lord!

MR. B: What you getting at, Rocky?

ROCKY: Let's face it, not everybody can be a Mr. B—but everybody can be strong in the Lord.

MR. B: I can see you're not gonna listen to Mr. B—so I'll just go and exercise my *own* muscles.

ROCKY: You need to go to the Bible and exercise your faith.

MR. B: You know, exercising makes my muscles grow.

ROCKY: Exercising your faith helps you grow in the Lord.

MR. B (*grunts*): Oh, no!

ROCKY: What's the matter?

MR. B: I can't move.

ROCKY: Why not?

MR. B: I finally put on so many gold chains—they're weighing me down! (*Grunts.*) I can't move.

ROCKY: Don't worry, B old buddy—Rocky to the rescue! (*He starts to leave.*)

MR. B: Hey! Where you going?

ROCKY: To get a tow truck—ha, ha, ha, ha.

(*Rocky exits and Mr. B sinks, groaning, out of sight.*)

59. Respect

(*The turkey and Mr. B enter.*)

TURKEY: Hey, there, this is Mr. T the turkey coming at you. And I've got a real problem. I don't get no respect. No respect at all. I'm a disgrace to my species. All my fellow turkeys avoid me. I had one guy tell me I wouldn't even make a decent TV dinner! I'll tell you, no respect at all. So I've decided to seek out a little help. I happen to run across this guy walking down the street—now he looks like the type that gets respect. Maybe he'll help me out and give me some advice.

MR. B: Are you talking about me?!

TURKEY: Yeah, but don't get riled up about it. I'll go away if you want me to, you know what I mean? You're the kind of guy I wouldn't want to run into in a dark alley. Come to think of it, I wouldn't want to run into you in broad open daylight. I'd rather risk insulting a grizzly bear, if you know what I mean.

MR. B: You talk too much, Turkey.

TURKEY: Whatever you say.

MR. B: And what you're saying is all wrong! Everything you say is negative!

TURKEY: That's because my life is negative.

MR. B: You need to change your thinking. You need a better self-image.

TURKEY: Maybe if I wore some gold chains like you, I'd get some respect. I was going to work out and build up my body, too—but they kicked me out of the health spa. They said having me around was bad for their image. I told them I wanted to pump iron and build up some muscles. They looked me over and said I couldn't even pump aluminum! Boy, I'll tell you. . . .

MR. B: You listen to me! It's not the gold chains or the muscles on the outside that count—it's what's on the inside. And if you're a Christian, you've got Jesus on the inside—and He's the Lord of lords, and King of kings!

TURKEY: I don't know.

MR. B: You gotta get rid of that loser mentality! You're a winner!

TURKEY: I am not a winner!

MR. B: Are you calling me a liar?!

TURKEY: No! No! What I mean is, I don't *feel* like a winner!

MR. B: You don't go by feelings, Turkey! You go by what the Bible says. Now you repeat after me, "I can do all things through Christ who strengthens me."

TURKEY: "I can do all things through Christ who strengthens me."

MR. B: "I give you not the spirit of fear, but of power, and of love, and of a sound mind."

TURKEY: "I give you not the spirit of fear, but of power, and of love, and of a sound mind."

MR. B: "Not by might, nor by power, but by my Spirit, says the Lord of hosts."

TURKEY: "Not by might, nor by power, but by my Spirit, says the Lord of hosts."

MR. B: "The righteous are as bold as a lion."

TURKEY: "The righteous are as bold as a lion."

MR. B: Now, are you beginning to believe it?

TURKEY: Yeah. . . .

MR. B: You keep repeating those scriptures and believe them! They're for us to live by. It's important to believe in God and believe in the Bible—and if you'll do that, you'll also believe in yourself! God didn't create any junk! You're God's masterpiece! Say it!

TURKEY (*in a wimpy voice*): I'm God's masterpiece.

MR. B: Say it and believe it! And you'll be able to walk with your head high and your shoulders straight.

TURKEY: But what about those people who are constantly picking on me?

MR. B: Don't base the way you feel about yourself on what they say. You're special because you belong to God. People who pick on you are just trying to build themselves up because *they* feel insecure and inadequate. So remember, come to Jesus. And if you're a born loser, He can make you a born-again winner. No one can out-class a child of the King!

TURKEY: Then maybe I'll get respect—just like you.

MR. B: Don't try to be like me. There's only one me. And there's only one you. You be the best turkey you can be. And then you'll get respect. You be yourself. Don't be a copycat or you'll just blend in with the crowd. Be a stand-out and stand up for Jesus.

TURKEY: I'm beginning to see your point. But then, anybody as big as you, I tend to listen to, you know what I mean? . . . This is Mr. T the turkey . . . and friend . . . saying so long.

(*The turkey and Mr. B exit.*)

60.
Turkey Parts

(*The cashier and the turkey enter.*)

CASHIER: Hello sir, and welcome to Fast Food Delight. May I help you?

TURKEY: I don't know. I'll tell you, I get no respect—no respect at all.

CASHIER: Is that a fact?

TURKEY: That's right. Everywhere I go—no respect at all. The other day I went over to Wendy's, and the man behind the counter looked at *me* and said, "Where's the beef?" I said, "Hey, I'm not a cow!" and he said, "You're not much of a turkey either!" I'll tell you, no respect at all!

CASHIER: Well, you'll never be rejected at Fast Food Delight!

TURKEY: Why is that?

CASHIER: Because we need the business. Parts is parts and business is business.

TURKEY: That's what I thought! You're after my money! Just once I wish someone would accept me without any wrong motives!

CASHIER: But, sir, I know someone who will accept you just the way you are, and His motives are the best.

TURKEY: Who's that?

CASHIER: Jesus Christ!

TURKEY: Jesus?

CASHIER: That's right. Jesus said, "Anyone who comes to me, I will never cast out or reject." And He also said, "I will never leave you nor forsake you."

TURKEY: Hey, that sounds like a pretty good offer to me.

CASHIER: Jesus has the best offer in town. But, unfortunately, He doesn't do much business either.

TURKEY: Why is that?

CASHIER: Mainly because people don't know what's on His menu. He has love, joy, peace, forgiveness, healing—and many other delicious items.

TURKEY: Maybe He should do more advertising.

CASHIER: I'm afraid that's up to us. Unless we advertise who Jesus is and what He has to offer, people will never know that life with the Lord tastes good. The Bible says, "Oh, taste and see, the Lord is good!"

TURKEY: I've got it! Maybe we could have a national taste test! I can see it now! "Four out of five people tested say life with Jesus tastes better than life in the world!"

CASHIER: But you'd have to remember that sin tastes mighty good for a season—but it soon gives an indigestion that not even Rolaids will help. The only way to really spell relief is J-E-S-U-S.

TURKEY: You know, Jesus sounds like me. He gets no respect, no respect at all!

CASHIER: That's very true. He gets very little respect now, but one day very soon, every knee shall bow, and every tongue will confess that Jesus is Lord and King forever and ever.

TURKEY: Amen to that! I can dig it!

CASHIER: And you know something else about the Lord's menu—He loves to give double portions!

TURKEY: What's that?

CASHIER: It's like a giant double-cheese burger—filled with the delights of Christian living!

TURKEY: Sounds pretty tasty to me.

CASHIER: Speaking of tasty, perhaps you'd like to try our new golden fried turkey made from 100 percent real parts of turkey.

TURKEY: Hey, do I look like the kind of bird that would betray my fellow turkeys?! Boy, I get no respect, no respect at all!

(*The cashier and turkey exit.*)

61.
The Bridge

(*Heathcliff the dragon, and a boy enter from opposite directions.*)

HEATHCLIFF: Halt! Stop! Woa! Desist! Not another step! Don't go any further!

BOY: Heathcliff, what are you doing?

HEATHCLIFF: I'm guarding this bridge, and nobody can cross it!

BOY: Why not?

HEATHCLIFF: Because I won't let them!

BOY: Why not?

HEATHCLIFF: Because I just read in a story book that dragons used to guard bridges and keep people from passing over them all the time.

BOY: Why did they do that?

HEATHCLIFF: Because they were mean, that's why.

BOY: But, Heathcliff, you're not mean. You're a good dragon.

HEATHCLIFF: Shhhh! Be quiet! What are you trying to do? Ruin my reputation?

BOY: So you're just going to stand here all day and keep people from crossing this bridge?

HEATHCLIFF: That's right. I have to be true to my heritage as a dragon.

BOY: You know what?

HEATHCLIFF: What?

BOY: You remind me of some Christians I know.

HEATHCLIFF: What do you mean?

BOY: You see this bridge we're on? It leads from one side of the park to the other side.

HEATHCLIFF: That's right. What about it?

BOY: You know what's on the other side of the park, don't you?

HEATHCLIFF: What?

BOY: The playground.

HEATHCLIFF: Oh, yeah. But what's that got to do with Christians?

BOY: Some Christians I know are guarding a bridge that leads to something very beautiful. And they won't let anybody cross it.

HEATHCLIFF: Really? It is the Golden Gate Bridge that leads to San Francisco? I've heard that's a beautiful place.

BOY: Nope.

HEATHCLIFF: What about the Brooklyn Bridge that leads to New York City?

BOY: No, no!

HEATHCLIFF: Than what bridge are they guarding?

BOY: They're guarding the bridge that leads from sin and death and problems, to forgiveness, life eternal, and the answer to those problems.

HEATHCLIFF: Wow! No kidding?

BOY: That's right. They're guarding that bridge by not telling anybody about it!

HEATHCLIFF: That's not very nice! What's the name of that bridge?

BOY: The name of the bridge ... is Jesus Christ. He's the bridge to peace, and joy, and deliverance—the bridge to God. He connects man back to a loving, heavenly Father.

HEATHCLIFF: And Jesus is the bridge over troubled waters!

BOY: Now you're getting it, Heathcliff! All Christians everywhere need to spread the word about God's healing love and forgiveness and help through Jesus. We need to tell people all about Jesus—our friends, our neighbors, and especially those who are hurting.

HEATHCLIFF: I see what you mean .... You know what?

BOY: What?

HEATHCLIFF: I'm getting bored. It's no fun guarding an old bridge all day long.

BOY: Then why don't we cross over to the other side and head to the playground?

HEATHCLIFF: That's a good idea. And maybe we'll find somebody there who we can tell about the Jesus bridge!

BOY: Maybe so, Heathcliff! Let's go find out!

(*Heathcliff and the boy exit.*)

62.
Little Jimmy

NARRATOR: Once upon a time there was a mean boy named Little Jimmy.

(*Jimmy enters.*)

JIMMY: I'm a mean boy!

NARRATOR: Yes—Little Jimmy was very, very mean.

MOM'S VOICE: Jimmy! Time for supper!

JIMMY (*challenging*): If you want me, come and get me!

NARRATOR: One day Little Jimmy was playing all by himself—mainly because no one else would play with him.

JIMMY: Oh yeah? Well, I don't need anybody else! I can have fun all by myself! (*A girl enters.*) Hey, you!

GIRL: Yes?

JIMMY: How come?

GIRL: How come what?

JIMMY: How come you got a face ... like a frog? Ha! Ha! Ha!

GIRL: I do not!

JIMMY: You do so!

GIRL: Do you always say mean things like that to people?

JIMMY: I say what I want and do as I please!

GIRL: But are you happy?

JIMMY: What do you mean? Of course I'm happy!

GIRL: You don't look very happy to me.

JIMMY: Well, who asked you?

GIRL: You poor little boy. I'll bet no one will be your friend because you're so mean.

JIMMY: So who cares if I don't have any friends? Who needs them?

GIRL: But you *do* have a friend. Everybody has got at least *one* friend.

JIMMY: Oh, yeah? Well, you tell me who that friend is, frogface!

GIRL: God is your friend.

JIMMY: What? You're crazy! Everybody knows that God likes good little boys and hates bad little boys!

GIRL: But that's not true! Jesus came to the earth and died on the cross so He could save *bad* people ... and be their friend.

JIMMY: You mean to tell me ... that the Lord did all that ... just to be my friend?

GIRL: That's right. I used to be just like you. But now that God is my friend, I can be a friend to everyone! And I'm not so mean anymore.

JIMMY: Wait a minute. *You'll* be my friend?

GIRL: Sure! And I'll introduce you to another friend—the Lord.

JIMMY: How will you do that?

GIRL: Well ... how about coming to church with me and my family this Sunday?

JIMMY: Aw ... I don't know about this church stuff.

GIRL: You're not scared, are you?

JIMMY: I'm not afraid of anybody or anything! I'll be there!

(*Jimmy and the girl exit.*)

NARRATOR: One day, a few months later, a remarkable change had taken place in Jimmy's life.

MOM'S VOICE: Jimmy! Time for supper!

(*Jimmy enters holding a rose.*)

JIMMY: Sure, Mom! And look what I've got for you today!

MOM'S VOICE: Oh, Jimmy, a rose! ... You're such a sweet boy.

JIMMY: Thanks, Mom ... (*He looks up.*) And thank you, Lord.

NARRATOR: And Little Jimmy lived *happily* ever after.

(*Jimmy exits.*)

63.
Heathcliff,
the Christmas Dragon

(*Heathcliff the dragon enters.*)

HEATHCLIFF: Oh, boy, Christmas is just around the corner! (*Looks around the corner.*) Yep! It's around there all right! Right around the corner! How I love Christmas! My favorite holiday of the year! How I love those bright lights, Christmas trees, and Christmas carols!

(*Gabriel, the angel enters.*)

GABRIEL: Hello there, Heathcliff.

HEATHCLIFF: Yipes! Who are you?

GABRIEL: I'm your guardian angel.

HEATHCLIFF: No kidding? Wow! What can I do for you?

GABRIEL: I have a special mission for you—from the Lord!

HEATHCLIFF: A special mission from the Lord?

GABRIEL: That's right. The Lord felt that you were just the man—I mean, dragon—for the job.

HEATHCLIFF: Sure! I'll do anything for the Lord! What's up?

GABRIEL: There is a young boy named Bobby Evans who doesn't understand the real meaning of Christmas. And unless you can teach him what Christmas is really about, his next door neighbor, a young boy named Hermie, isn't going to have Christmas at all this year.

HEATHCLIFF: Why not?

GABRIEL: Hermie's father is out of work, and his mother is very sick in the hospital. Bobby Evans holds the key to helping Hermie and his family. But first, Bobby has to understand what Christmas is really all about. Think you can handle that assignment?

HEATHCLIFF: Sure! I'll be the Lord's secret agent!

Where does Bobby Evans live?

GABRIEL: 211 Westchester.

HEATHCLIFF: I'm on my way!

(*Heathcliff and Gabriel exit. Bobby and his mother enter from opposite directions.*)

MOTHER: Oh, Bobby—

BOBBY: Yes, Mother?

MOTHER: You know that Christmas is just around the corner.

BOBBY: It sure is!

MOTHER: Well, how about giving me some idea of what you want for Christmas?

BOBBY: Sure! Let's see . . . I want a G.I. Joe Persuader, a G.I. Joe Sea Ray, a G.I. Joe Night Raven, and a G.I. Joe Tomahawk 'Copter.

MOTHER: Oh, my!

BOBBY: Wait a minute! I'm not finished yet! I also want a new baseball and a baseball bat, a basketball, some boxing gloves, a remote-controlled racecar, a Hot Wheels daredevil racetrack, a train set, an official Miami Dolphins sweatshirt, an electric bowling game, some ice skates, a hockey stick, a ten-speed bicycle, a moped, a telescope, a microscope, an insect-dissection kit, some cowboy boots, a swingset for our backyard. . . .

MOTHER: Hold it! How much more is there?

BOBBY: Oh, I guess that's all. I'll let you get by with that this year.

MOTHER: Well, your father and I will see what we can do.

(*Mother exits.*)

BOBBY (*singing*): Toys! I'm gonna get toys! Oh, boy! I'm gonna get toys!

(*Hermie enters.*)

HERMIE: Hey, Bobby! Watcha singing about?

BOBBY: Hi there, Hermie! I'm singing about toys! All the toys I'm gonna get for Christmas.

BOBBY (*sadly*): You're lucky. I don't think I'm getting anything this Christmas.

BOBBY: Oh? That's too bad. Well, better luck next year! (*Hermie exits. Bobby sings.*) Toys! I'm gonna get toys! Oh, boy! I'm gonna get toys!

(*Heathcliff enters.*)

HEATHCLIFF: Now is that any way to treat your best friend?

BOBBY: Yipes! Who are you? And *what* are you?

HEATHCLIFF (*singing*): I'm Heathcliff the Christmas dragon!

BOBBY: Sure you are! And I'm the Easter bunny! Ha! Ha! Ha!

HEATHCLIFF: Never mind that! How could you be so uncaring about Hermie?

BOBBY: What do you mean?

HEATHCLIFF: Didn't you hear him? He's not getting *anything* for Christmas—and you're getting all those toys! And you didn't even offer to give him any.

BOBBY: Give him some of my toys? Are you crazy? What for?

HEATHCLIFF: Don't you know what Christmas is all about?

BOBBY: Sure! It's getting presents and gifts and toys and games ... and unwrapping boxes, and eating fruit cakes and cookies....

HEATHCLIFF: No, no! Christmas is *giving!*

BOBBY: Giving?

HEATHCLIFF: On the very first Christmas, God gave the whole world a gift, the most precious gift He could give—His very own Son. God so loved the world that He gave His only Son to die for us, so that we could be saved from our sin.

BOBBY: Yeah, I know all that. But what has that got to do with Hermie?

HEATHCLIFF: Look at poor Hermie. His father out of work, his mother sick ... no Christmas tree, no toys, and his Christmas dinner will probably be a can of soup!

BOBBY: But what can *I* do?

HEATHCLIFF: Maybe if you'd give up a few of your toys, and ask your mom and dad to help Hermie and his family instead—

BOBBY: I don't know ...

(*A devil puppet enters.*)

DEVIL: No! Don't do it!

BOBBY: I hear this strange voice telling me not to do it.

HEATHCLIFF: Don't listen to it! It's the devil!

DEVIL: Don't do it, Bobby! Think of all those toys! Think of the fun you'll have! You can have anything you want! Anything!

HEATHCLIFF: Think of Hermie! He's your friend! What if you were in his place?

DEVIL: Never mind Hermie! Who cares about him? Think of yourself! Think of all those toys! Mountains of toys! Oh, boy!

HEATHCLIFF: Well, Bobby? What do you say? Remember, Christmas is giving. And God has already given you His gift of Jesus.

BOBBY: I'll do it! I'll help out Hermie and his family!

DEVIL: No! No! Don't do it!

HEATHCLIFF: Shut up, you old devil!

DEVIL: You can't make me shut up!

(*Gabriel enters.*)

GABRIEL: Yes he can!

DEVIL: Yipes! It's the heavenly police! I'm getting outta here!

(*The devil exits.*)

BOBBY: Hey, Mom!

(*Mother enters.*)

MOTHER: Yes, Bobby?

BOBBY: Forget about all those toys! Let's help out Hermie and his family instead! Let's invite them over for Christmas dinner.

MOTHER: Oh, Bobby, what a wonderful idea! Of course we will!

BOBBY: You think we can pick out a few toys for Hermie? You can forget about some of mine.

MOTHER: I think there will be presents for *both* of you under the tree this year.

BOBBY: Oh, boy! Let's go tell Hermie!

(*Bobby and his mother exit.*)

GABRIEL: Congratulations, Heathcliff! Well done! The Lord is very pleased.

HEATHCLIFF: Well, praise the Lord!

GABRIEL: What are *your* plans for Christmas this year?

HEATHCLIFF: I'm going to Scotland to visit my cousin—the Loch Ness monster ... Why do you ask?

GABRIEL: Because I'm your guardian angel—I go everywhere you go.

HEATHCLIFF: No kidding?

GABRIEL: That's right.

HEATHCLIFF: Then let's go back to my place, and I'll fix us both a cup of hot chocolate.

GABRIEL: All right! Let's go!

HEATHCLIFF & GABRIEL (*In unison*): Merry Christmas everybody! So long!

(*Heathcliff and Gabriel exit.*)

64. Dragon Power

(*A boy enters.*)

BOY: Hi, everybody! I'm here today to talk about *power*. You know, there are many different kinds of power. There's electric power, steam power, solar power, nuclear power, wind power, gasoline power. . . .

(*Heathcliff enters.*)

HEATHCLIFF: Don't forget—dragon power!

BOY: Oh, yeah—Dragon power . . . *Dragon power?!!!*

HEATHCLIFF: Rawrr! *That's* dragon power!

BOY: Your breath sure is hot, Mr. Dragon.

HEATHCLIFF: Must be the chili peppers I had for lunch. And the name is Heathcliff—not "Mr. Dragon."

BOY: Sure! Anything you say! You've . . . already had lunch, then?

HEATHCLIFF: That's right. Take it easy, kid. I don't eat people!

BOY: You don't? Well, what do you eat—besides chili peppers?

HEATHCLIFF: Well, being a fire-breathing dragon, I love TV dinners. You just heat 'n eat!

BOY: Oh. What's your favorite TV dinner?

HEATHCLIFF: Magnavox.

BOY: Magnavox?

HEATHCLIFF: Yep! Zeniths are yummy, too! And Panasonics are great with a touch of mustard.

BOY: You eat television sets?!

HEATHCLIFF: Sure! But lately I've been on a diet, so I've been eating only portables.

BOY: Yeech! I could never eat a television set.

HEATHCLIFF: That's because you're a puny little kid! You eat stuff like Cream of Wheat and candy bars! But I'm a big, powerful dragon! I'm so powerful I could lick Hulk Hogan! *You* couldn't even lick a lollipop!

BOY: I am not a puny little kid! I've got power too!

HEATHCLIFF: Oh, yeah? What kind of power?

BOY: Kid power!

HEATHCLIFF: What's kid power?

BOY: It's the power you get when you know the Word of God. Like David when he faced Goliath. He looked pretty puny next to that giant. But he believed the Word of God, so God gave little David the power to slay Goliath.

HEATHCLIFF: A kid named David slew a giant? How'd he do it?

BOY: With a rock.

HEATHCLIFF: With a rock? He must've been pretty close to the guy.

BOY: You could say he was only a ... stone's throw away! Ha! Ha! Ha!

HEATHCLIFF: You tell crummy jokes, kid. But I like your spunk. How do I get some of this kid power.

BOY: You have to become a child of God, and then learn what the scriptures say. For example, Jesus loves children. And He once said that unless you become like a little child, you can't enter the Kingdom of Heaven.

HEATHCLIFF: I have to become like a child, huh? Does that mean I have to eat Cream of Wheat—yueech!

BOY: No! It means you have to accept Jesus and love and trust Him the way a child loves and trusts his parents. Think you can do that?

HEATHCLIFF: Well, I don't know. You might have to teach me how.

BOY: I'd be glad to.

HEATHCLIFF: Great! How about coming home with me for dinner?

BOY: Well, uh.... What are you having?

HEATHCLIFF: How about a Sony? "Sony no baloney!" I love Japanese food. We can use the antennas as chopsticks!

BOY: I think I'll stick to Cream of Wheat!

HEATHCLIFF: Sure, kid! (*Laughs.*) Anything you want! Let's go!

(*Heathcliff and the boy exit.*)

65.
Dragonslayer

(*Heathcliff and a man enter from opposite directions.*)

MAN: Excuse me, sir, tell me — are you a dragon?

HEATHCLIFF: No — I'm a porcupine! Ha! Ha! Ha!

MAN: Really? I must say, you certainly look like a dragon.

HEATHCLIFF: Of course I'm a dragon!

MAN: Oh, splendid! Are you a real, live, fire-breathing dragon?

HEATHCLIFF: Well, I don't breathe fire — unless I've just had lunch at Taco John's.

MAN: Well, I guess you'll do then.

HEATHCLIFF: Do for what?

MAN: I just wish you could be a little more threatening.

HEATHCLIFF: What are you talking about?

MAN: I'm going to have to slay you.

HEATHCLIFF: Slay me!

MAN: Yes — but don't take it personally.

HEATHCLIFF: But why do you want to slay me?

MAN: Well, you see, my name is Percy Hicklebee. And I'm a nobody.

HEATHCLIFF: A what?

MAN: A nobody. You see, I've never done anything special. Not ever. I've been Mr. Average

all my life. You know what I mean?

HEATHCLIFF: Not exactly.

MAN: I've always been just another face in the crowd. I've never won anything, my grades were always average in school. I'm not very good looking. I've never had many friends. I'm just a nobody. A big zero.

HEATHCLIFF: Well, what's that got to do with slaying a dragon?

MAN: Well, I figure if I slay a dragon, I'll be a hero! A real, live, genuine hero! I'll be a somebody! People will look up to me! I will have done something important! Who knows, maybe they'll even make me a royal knight! Sir Percy Hicklebee! I like the sound of that, I must say!

HEATHCLIFF: Wait a minute. I think you're going about this all wrong.

MAN: What do you mean?

HEATHCLIFF: You don't have to slay a dragon to be somebody important. You're already somebody important!

MAN: You're just trying to talk me out of slaying you, right? I've heard you dragons are tricky critters.

HEATHCLIFF: No, no, I'm not jiving you. You really are someone special.

MAN: I am not! Nobody has ever told me that.

HEATHCLIFF: Have you ever asked God how *He* feels about you?

MAN: Well, no....

HEATHCLIFF: Just think, He created you *totally* unique! From the top of your head to the tips of your toes, there's not another person like you in the whole world!

MAN: I've never thought of that.

HEATHCLIFF: Speaking of thoughts, nobody thinks like you do, or sees things like you do. Nobody reasons like you do. And nobody does exactly the same things you do.

MAN: I'm beginning to see what you mean. I'm special because I'm unique.

HEATHCLIFF: Exactly! You don't have to win worldly prizes to be special. God has already made you special. The Bible says we are all gloriously and wonderfully made by Him.

MAN: But my life is so boring, so average.

HEATHCLIFF: But God has a special, unique, and exciting plan for your life. A mission that only you—Percy Hicklebee—can carry out.

MAN: Really?

HEATHCLIFF: That's right! But you have to turn your life over to Him to find out the plan.

MAN: But will it be as exciting as slaying dragons?

HEATHCLIFF: There's a dragon out there called the devil. And *his* strongholds need to be attacked and conquered.

MAN: But ... will they make me a knight?

HEATHCLIFF: You'll be more than a knight! When you come into the Lord's family, you're coming into the King's family. And that will make you a *prince!* And one day you'll be crowned with more glory and honor than you could ever dream of!

MAN: That sounds like just what I'm looking for! When can I start?

HEATHCLIFF: Right away! Just give your life to Jesus and let Him train you a little bit with the Word of God.

MAN: Is that training business really necessary?

HEATHCLIFF: You don't go into the boxing ring with an experienced fighter like the devil without training for it.

MAN: I suppose you're right. That makes sense.

HEATHCLIFF: But one day soon, you'll be ready for him! And from the moment you give yourself to Jesus, God will be on your side backing you up!

MAN: Thank you for straightening me out. I must say, this conversation has been very enlightening.

HEATHCLIFF: Well, it sure beats getting shish kebabed!

MAN: Look out, devil! Here I come! Percy Hicklebee has joined God's army!

(*Heathcliff and the man exit.*)

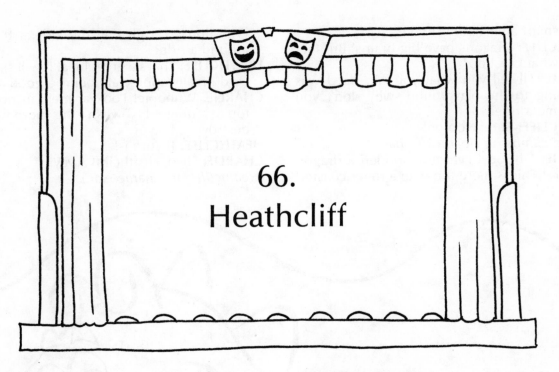

66.
Heathcliff

(*Charlie enters.*)

CHARLIE: Oh, boy! What a beautiful day! What could possibly go wrong on a beautiful day like today?

(*Heathcliff enters.*)

HEATHCLIFF: Rawrr!

CHARLIE: Oh, no! It's a dragon! Help! Help! Run for your lives! It's a dragon!

HEATHCLIFF (*scared*): A dragon! Oh, no! Where? Where?

CHARLIE: What do you mean, where? *You're* the dragon!

HEATHCLIFF: Oh! Say, don't scare me like that! I was ready to head for the hills!

CHARLIE: Are you gonna eat me, Mr. Dragon?

HEATHCLIFF: Of course not! I only eat health foods—and you don't look very healthy to me.

CHARLIE: For a dragon, you sure don't sound very mean.

HEATHCLIFF: I'm as gentle as a puppy! I wouldn't hurt a daisy!

CHARLIE: What brings you here, Mr. Dragon?

HEATHCLIFF: I just wanted to say hello. I saw you as I was *draggin'* down the highway. Ha! Ha! Get it? *Draggin'* down the highway!

CHARLIE: Oh, no. . . .

HEATHCLIFF: Sorry, kid. . . .

CHARLIE: I'm sure glad you're not a fire-breathing dragon—you could have barbecued me!

HEATHCLIFF: I don't like barbecue—it makes me burp. And when a *dragon* burps, you better stand back. But I sure wish I *was* a mean, fire-breathing dragon!

CHARLIE: Why?

HEATHCLIFF: Because! I just don't like being so meek and shy! Just once I'd like to go on a rampage like Godzilla and destroy a city!

CHARLIE: Oh, no, you mustn't think that! You should be thankful that God made you the way you are! You're really unique! There aren't enough gentle dragons in the world! You're a real standout! Almost one-of-a-kind!

HEATHCLIFF: Really? I'd never thought of it that way.

CHARLIE: That's right! My name is Charlie, and I consider it a great honor to meet such a rare specimen of a dragon!

HEATHCLIFF: Well, my name is Heathcliff! And it's a pleasure to meet you, too.

CHARLIE: You know, you ought to thank the Lord that He made you so unique!

HEATHCLIFF: You're right! I think I will! Thank you, Lord! How was that?

CHARLIE: Well, it's a start. But what have you done lately to show the Lord your appreciation?

HEATHCLIFF: What do you mean? What can *I* do for the Lord? I'm just a lowly dragon.

CHARLIE: That may be so, but the Bible says "As you have done it unto the least of these, you have done it unto me."

HEATHCLIFF: In other words, doing something good for somebody else is like doing something good for the Lord?

CHARLIE: Exactly! You catch on quick! You're

a very smart animal, aren't you?

HEATHCLIFF: Dragons have big brains! But let's see, what can I do?

CHARLIE: I'll tell you what you can do! I was heading to the playground—why don't you give me a ride?

HEATHCLIFF: Sure! Hop on!

(*Charlie climbs on Heathcliff's back.*)

CHARLIE: Oh, boy! I've never ridden a dragon before! This is more fun than a roller coaster!

Why don't you give all the kids at the playground a ride?

HEATHCLIFF: That's a great idea! It will show the Lord I really appreciate being a good dragon!

CHARLIE: Whoopie! Look at me! I'm riding on top of a dragon! Now isn't this more fun than destroying Tokyo?

HEATHCLIFF: It sure is!

CHARLIE: Hiyo, Heathcliff! Away!

(*Heathcliff and Charlie exit.*)

67. Guardian Angels

(*Bertrum enters.*)

BERTRUM: Gabriel! Gabriel! Gabriel! Come out, come out, wherever you are!

(*Gabriel enters.*)

GABRIEL: Bertrum! You don't have to shout! They could probably hear you on the other side of Heaven!

BERTRUM: Sorry. I keep forgetting that angels have *big* voices.

GABRIEL: That's so we can announce *big* events! Like the birth of Jesus!

BERTRUM: Or the resurrection of Jesus!

GABRIEL: Or the second coming of Jesus!

BERTRUM: Or anything else that involves Jesus!

GABRIEL: So what did you want?

BERTRUM: I just wanted to tell you I'm all packed and ready to go. I've got my supplies and everything together. What about you?

GABRIEL: What are you talking about?

BERTRUM: Didn't you hear what the Lord said the other day? We're all going camping! Oh, boy! I can hardly wait!

GABRIEL: Camping?

BERTRUM: Yeah! And I'm ready! I've got everything! A fishing pole, a tent, a frying pan, a sleeping bag—

GABRIEL: Bertrum, angels don't sleep.

BERTRUM: Oh, yeah, I forgot. But that just means I'll have more time to enjoy the trip! I've even got some marshmallows and Beanie Wienies!

GABRIEL: Bertrum, I don't know about you sometimes.

BERTRUM: What do you mean? The only thing the Lord didn't say was where we were going. Maybe we'll see the Grand Canyon, or visit the mountains of Colorado, or maybe go to Yosemite National Park. Do you think we'll see Yogi Bear? Yabba dabba do!

GABRIEL: Bertrum, we're not going camping!

BERTRUM: We're not?

GABRIEL: No. The Lord said that some angels would be *encamping* themselves around Christians—just like it says in the Bible.

BERTRUM: What does that mean?

GABRIEL: We're going to be setting up and living close by some Christians so we can better protect and guide them.

BERTRUM: Ohhhhh. We're going to *be guarding* them.

GABRIEL: That's right. That's part of our job as guardian angels. Whenever someone accepts the Lord, we're sent on the scene to help them out.

BERTRUM: And we also look after the children. Boy, is that a tough job! Seems like those kids are always getting into trouble!

GABRIEL: You can say that again, Bertrum.

BERTRUM: It's too bad that people can't see us in action—they'd feel a lot more secure in the Lord.

GABRIEL: People do see us from time to time. Remember when we surrounded the prophet Elisha in chariots of fire to protect him from his enemies?

BERTRUM: Yeah, I remember that! Oh, oh!

GABRIEL: What's wrong?

BERTRUM: I feel a dance coming on! All right! Let's cut loose!

(Bertrum sings and dances.)

GABRIEL: Bertrum! What are you doing?

BERTRUM: Someone just accepted the Lord down on the earth! Someone just got saved! And whenever that happens, it says in the Bible that the angels in Heaven rejoice! So I'm just doing my job!

GABRIEL: I know it says that, but would you try acting more like an angel?

BERTRUM: And how does an angel act?

GABRIEL: *Dignified.*

BERTRUM: Well, exxxxcccuuussseee me!

GABRIEL: Except when we're around the devil and his crowd—then we act like *Rambo!*

BERTRUM: All right! Go ahead, devil, make my day!

GABRIEL: I've got some divine business to attend to, Bertum, but I'll see you at the ... camp-out.

BERTRUM: I'll be there!

(Gabriel and Bertrum exit.)

NOW PLAYING →

68.
Gabriel and Bertrum

(*Bertrum the angel enters.*)

BERTRUM: Gabriel! Gabriel! Gabriel! Come quick! Come a running! Come a flying! Just get here!

(*Gabriel the angel enters.*)

GABRIEL: What is it, Bertrum?

BERTRUM: Is it time, yet? Is it time? Please tell me it's time!

GABRIEL: Time for what? Bertrum, control yourself!

BERTRUM: Time for what? Is it time for the Lord to return to the earth?!

GABRIEL: Not yet, Bertrum! Have patience! Calm down! Remember you're an angel! We're supposed to be dignified! You're acting all hyper—like a human being or something!

BERTRUM: Patience? Calm down? I can't calm down! Everyone in Heaven is running around all excited, and you say, "Calm down!"

GABRIEL: Bertrum, it will be very soon, I promise you. Very soon the Lord and all His angels are going to split open the sky and sweep across the earth! But we can't go yet!

BERTRUM: Why not?

GABRIEL: The Lord is waiting for more people to hear the gospel. It has to be preached all over the world. Every man, woman, and child needs to hear the good news that Jesus Christ has come to forgive their sins and freely give eternal life!

BERTRUM: You're right ... look out! (*A satellite flies by.*) I wish they'd watch where they're going with those satellites!

GABRIEL: Humans sure are strange. I don't know what they're looking for up here, anyway. You should see how excited they get over a couple of dusty old moon rocks!

BERTRUM: They need to get more excited over the rock of their salvation—Jesus Christ!

GABRIEL: Amen to that, Brother Bertrum!

BERTRUM: Is there any way we can hurry the Lord's return to the earth? The people don't know what they're missing!

GABRIEL: It's up to them, Bertrum. If they would get busy and preach this gospel, and go all-out to reach their neighbors and friends—who knows? They might just speed things up a bit!

BERTRUM: Let's go tell them the wonderful news!

GABRIEL: We're not supposed to tell them! Telling the good news is the human's job, and there are many ways and places they can tell it—including church, Sunday school, and vacation Bible school—and even puppet shows!

BERTRUM: I like puppet shows!

GABRIEL: It won't be long, Bertrum.

BERTRUM: I can hardly wait! When I see that beautiful heavenly city waiting up here with its gates of pearl and golden streets—shining and glowing in the light and glory of God, I get excited! Everyone in Heaven is excited! Just waiting for God's children on earth to join us for eternity!

GABRIEL: Just a little while longer and there will be no more sorrow, or pain, or poverty, or death! Only eternal life, eternal love, and eternal joy!

BERTRUM: Let's get this message preached! Before it's too late! Wait a minute!

GABRIEL: What is it?

BERTRUM: Did I just hear the Lord say ... *"It's time to go"*??!

GABRIEL: No, Bertrum. But it soon will be.

BERTRUM: Then let's get ready! There's no time to lose! I've got to press my robe!

GABRIEL: And I've got to practice my trumpet playing!

BERTRUM: Well, let's get going!

(*Gabriel and Bertrum exit.*)

69. The Lone Stranger

(The Lone Stranger and Pronto enter on stick horses.)

STRANGER: Hi yo, Silver, away!

(They ride around crashing into one another to the sound of the William Tell Overture. Finally, the music fades.)

STRANGER: Well, Pronto ... here we are in the roughest town in the West. Keep your eyes peeled for trouble.

PRONTO: Right, Kimo Sloppy.

STRANGER: How many times have I got to tell you! That's Kimo *Sobby*—not Kimo Sloppy!

PRONTO: Whatever you say, Kimo Sloppy. *(The Lone Stranger groans.)* Kimo Sloppy, I got question.

STRANGER: What is it, Pronto?

PRONTO: Why we always on the lookout for trouble?

STRANGER: Because we stand for truth, justice, and God's way.

PRONTO: Oh.

STRANGER: It's our way of serving mankind. We promote righteousness and law and order as we travel the wild, wild west.

PRONTO: I got another question for great white Lone Stranger.

STRANGER: What is it now?

PRONTO: Why you always wear that funny little mask? You like big raccoon.

STRANGER: It's my trademark! Every hero in the wild west has his own trademark. Buffalo Bill has his buffaloes, Sitting Bull has his bulls, I've got my mask and a horse named Sliver, Annie Oakley has her curly red hair and dog named Sandy ...

PRONTO: That is little Orphan Annie, Kimo Sloppy, not Annie Oakley.

STRANGER: Whatever! *(Mad Jack enters carrying tracts.)* Wait a minute, Pronto. Do my eyes deceive me? Isn't that Mad Jack McCoy?

PRONTO: Yes it is, Kimo Sloppy!

STRANGER: He's the meanest, roughest, toughest, most vile man in the entire West!

PRONTO: And he's heading this way! Let's get outta here.

STRANGER: No, Pronto, we're standing our ground! Just like Wyatt Earp at the OK corral, and General Grant at Appomattox....

PRONTO: And General Custer at Little Big Horn?

STRANGER: Quiet, Pronto, here he comes.

JACK: Howdy, Lone Stranger! I'd recognize that mask anywhere.

STRANGER: Don't you howdy me, Mad Jack! What kind of trouble are you stirring up?

JACK: I'm not causing any trouble—I'm just passing out these religious tracts here.

STRANGER: What?!

JACK: That's right, Lone Stranger, see ... Jesus Loves You, One Way to Heaven, and Jesus is the Answer.

STRANGER: Mad Jack, the last time I saw you was in a street fight. You took on three guys—and all three ended up in the hospital.

JACK: Yeah, I used to have a real bad temper. But now that I've been born again, the Lord has set me free from that. I used to hate everybody, but now I love them. You're looking at the new Jack McCoy.

PRONTO: Jack McCoy has become a Christian brother, Kimo Sloppy.

JACK: That's right, Pronto. A real blood brother through the blood of Jesus.

STRANGER: And now you're passing out tracts?

JACK: That's right. We've all got a job to do serving the Lord, and I've been given my job. Instead of tearing down communities like I used to, I'm trying to build them up now with the gospel.

STRANGER: Well, praise the Lord, Jack! Keep up the good work!

JACK: Thanks, Lone Stranger. See you later.

(Jack exits.)

STRANGER: Well, what do you know about that? Mad Jack McCoy following Christ and leading people to Jesus! What a turn-around!

(Pronto begins to dance and chant.)

STRANGER: Pronto, why are you doing a rain dance?

PRONTO: I not dancing, Kimo Sloppy! I just stepped on a cactus!

(More chanting.)

STRANGER: Control yourself, Pronto!

PRONTO: That easy for you to say! You have on your thick cowboy boots—I have to wear these little moccasins!

STRANGER: Well, Pronto, it looks like our work is done here. It's time to hit the trail and ride off into the sunset.

PRONTO: Ready when you are, Kimo Sloppy!

STRANGER: Hi yo, Silver! Away!

(They ride off to the sound of the William Tell Overture's ending.)

NOW PLAYING →

70.
The Lone Stranger II

(*The Lone Stranger and Pronto enter, accompanied by the music of the William Tell Overture*)

STRANGER: Hi yo, Silver! Away!

ANNOUNCER: Out of the wild and rugged West they rode—the Lone Stranger and Pronto. Fearless defenders of truth, justice, and God's way....

(*The music fades.*)

STRANGER: Well, Pronto, here we are on the Rio Grande.

PRONTO: Right, Kimo Sloppy!

STRANGER: I've told you a thousand times! That's Kimo *Sobby*—not Kimo *Sloppy!*

PRONTO: Whatever you say, Kimo Sloppy! (*The Lone Stranger groans.*) Kimo Sloppy, what are we doing here, so close to Mexico?

STRANGER: We're on the lookout for burritos, Pronto.

PRONTO: Burritos?

STRANGER: That's right. Wild, vicious, gunslinging burritos.

PRONTO: Uh ... I think you mean banditos, Kimo Sloppy. You get burritos at Taco Bell's.

STRANGER: Whatever! A Mexican bandit by any other name is still a Mexican bandit!

PRONTO: I think you need a vacation, Kimo Sloppy. I think you been riding open trail too long.

STRANGER: Let's change the subject, Pronto! (*The Taco Kid enters.*) Wait a minute, Pronto! Look over there! We're in for it now! I'd recognize that mustache anywhere.

PRONTO: You don't mean—!

STRANGER: Yes! The Taco Kid!

KID: Buenas nochas, senors.

STRANGER: Don't you "buenas nochas" me, Taco Kid! I know who you are! What low-down, mean, vicious, vile, conniving, evil, corrupt trouble are you up to now?

KID: I'm not causing any trouble.

STRANGER: But aren't you the infamous Mexican bandit they call the Taco Kid?

KID: I used to be. But I've changed my ways. Now I own a combination Mexican and seafood restaurant. I call it Taco Squid.

STRANGER: Taco Squid?!

KID: That's right! And we use only the freshest green squids in our tacos!

STRANGER & PRONTO: Bleeech!!

STRANGER: You mean to tell us that you're no longer rampaging across the countryside causing mass destruction?

KID: That's right. I no longer roam across the countryside. Now I live in a little hacienda on the prairie.

PRONTO: You've really changed.

KID: There was a time I was going my own way in life—and not getting anywhere. I was always getting into trouble, too. So one day I decided to follow the Lord and to make something of my life.

PRONTO: The Taco Kid has become a blood brother, Kimo Sloppy.

KID: That's right. Saved through the blood of Jesus. When I was younger I didn't follow the Lord. And I paid a terrible price for it. I had no peace, no love, no joy, no rest. But when I finally came to my senses, I turned to the Lord and found Him waiting for me with open arms. And I learned that the Lord has a wonderful plan for our lives. And if we follow Him, He'll unfold that plan for us. Well, I've got to be going now. It's time to cook the squids. Care to join me?

STRANGER: Uh ... maybe some other time.

KID: Whatever you say. Adios, amigos.

(*The Taco Kid exits.*)

STRANGER: Well, Pronto, it's time for us to hit the dusty trail again, too.

PRONTO: Why can't we use the freeway?

STRANGER: Because, it just wouldn't be right for two western heroes—legends in their own time!—to use the freeway.

PRONTO: Whatever you say, Kimo Sloppy.

STRANGER: Just follow me, Pronto.

PRONTO: I think I'll follow the Lord instead—at least He knows where He's going—and knows where I should go, too.

STRANGER: Right you are, Pronto! Hi yo, Silver! Away!

(*They ride off to the sound of the William Tell Overture's ending.*)

119

71.
Captain Redbeard

(Redbeard enters.)

REDBEARD (singing): Oh, he went out to sea and he never came back! He went out to sea and he never came back! He went out to sea and he never came back! He took a wrong turn and he never came back! Ha! Ha-ha-ha! Ha-ha-ho! Arrr, I love singing sea chanties! One of these days I'll be bigger than Elvis! Arrr, what a beautiful day to set sail. It warms me pirate's heart!

(The mate enters.)

MATE: Seaman Hicklebee, reporting for duty, sir!

REDBEARD: Don't interrupt me while I'm singing! Or I'll use you for shark bait!

MATE: S-s-sorry, s-s-sir!

REDBEARD: Are you the new first mate?

MATE: Yes, sir!

REDBEARD: Well, welcome aboard! I'm Captain Redbeard, the most feared pirate on the seven seas! What did you say your name is?

MATE: Percy, sir. Percy Hicklebee.

REDBEARD: That sure is a sissy name! … I'm going to change your name so you sound more like a pirate! From now on your name will be Billy Bones.

MATE: Whatever you say, sir. You're the captain.

REDBEARD: That's right. I'm the captain of this ship, and you take your orders from me. When I say, "Hoist the sails!" you hoist the sails. When I say, "Scrub the cannons!" you scrub the cannons. Understand?

MATE: Yes, sir!

REDBEARD: Then you're a lot smarter than you look! If you're ever going to get anywhere in this life, or learn anything, you've got to obey and respect those who are older and wiser than you are. Every person who wants to go his or her own way, do his own thing, and

think he knows it all, will end up shipwrecked on the rocks of life every time!

MATE: Yes, sir.

REDBEARD: You obey my orders, and I'll turn you from a sissy into a first-class pirate.

MATE: But I don't want to be a pirate.

REDBEARD: What? Then why did you sign on with a pirate ship?!

MATE: I thought this was the Love Boat!

REDBEARD: Oh, no!

MATE: You want to play some shuffleboard?

REDBEARD: No, I don't want to play some shuffleboard! Listen, you just obey my orders and I'll turn you into a real sailor! Understand?

MATE: Yes, sir! What are your first orders, sir?

REDBEARD: I want you to swab the poop deck until you poop out!

MATE: Aye-aye, sir!

(The mate exits.)

REDBEARD: Arrr! Imagine thinking this was the Love Boat! How stupid can you be? Now where was I? Oh, yeah! Sea chanties! (Starts to sing.) Ohhh—

(The lieutenant enters.)

LT: Lieutenant Shem, reporting for duty, sir!

REDBEARD: Don't interrupt me while I'm singing! Or I'll make you walk the plank! Who are you, anyway?

LT: I'm the new first lieutenant!

REDBEARD: Welcome aboard, matey!

(Several animal puppets pop up.)

REDBEARD: Wait a minute! What are all those animals doing on board?!

LT: I brought them on board, sir!

REDBEARD: What for?!

LT: What for? You mean this isn't Noah's Ark?

REDBEARD: No! It's a pirate ship! I give up!

(They all exit.)

72. Good News

(*Walter enters.*)

WALTER: Hello and welcome to the daily news report. I'm your anchorman, Walter Concrete. Today's headlines include a reported increase in wars, famines, pestilence, disease, poverty, and crime all over the world. Earthquakes, active volcanoes, tidal waves, flooding, and droughts have taken a heavy toll today, monsoons and hurricanes are doing heavy damage, and forest fires are raging out of control in several areas. And now for the really bad news; unemployment continues to rise along with interest rates, thefts and robberies are up, and more corruption has been uncovered in high places. In other words, just another typical day on planet earth. And now we'll take you for close-up reports the world over from our many correspondents—live via satellite, in living color, so you can see for yourself just how terrible things really are today ... wait a minute! That does it! Hold everything!

(*The director enters.*)

DIRECTOR (*very upset*): Walter, what is it? Excuse us, folks, we're having technical problems, please stand by.

WALTER: I'm not having technical problems!

DIRECTOR: What's wrong? Did you loose your script? Just read the teleprompter!

WALTER: I didn't loose my script! I'm just fed up with it!

DIRECTOR: Walter, what are you doing? This is a live newscast! Millions of people are watching and listening!

WALTER: I don't care! I'm not going to report any more bad news! I'm sick of it!

DIRECTOR: Murray, cut to a commercial quick! And get a doctor—Walter's gone bananas!

WALTER: Don't you dare cut to a commercial! I want to be heard!

DIRECTOR: Walter, you *are* being heard, coast-to-coast and around the world! We're the highest-rated news show on television! So come through for us, read the news, and let's get on with the broadcast.

WALTER: You mean the people out there really want to hear all this garbage?

DIRECTOR: Garbage! We've got the best reporters on television. They search high and low for the latest news.

WALTER: Well, they've sure missed a lot today!

DIRECTOR: What do you mean? Do you know something? Walter, do you have a scoop? Is that what all this is about?

WALTER: You bet I've got a scoop! Did you ever stop and think about all the *good* things that have happened today?

DIRECTOR: Good things? What are you talking about?

WALTER: Somebody helped someone today. Someone spoke a kind word, and helped to lift another's burden. Someone gave of their time and money to a charity. Somebody visited someone in the hospital.

DIRECTOR: Walter that's not news! News is a bomb going off, a house burning down....

WALTER: I'm tired of reporting only bad news! I say, let's give equal time to good news! No wonder everybody's depressed!

DIRECTOR: I give up! Just report something! We're still on the air!

WALTER: Hello, and welcome to the Good News report. I'm your anchorman, Walter Concrete. All over the world today, Jesus Christ entered human hearts and changed lives. Families were brought back together by the love of God. Miracles of healing took place by the power of the Holy Spirit. Dedicated Christians tore down many of Satan's strongholds today. And the church of God continues to unify and become strong. Somewhere, the gospel was preached to someone who'd never heard it before. In other places, impossible situations and problems were solved and conquered through faith in Jesus Christ. Angels were hard at work today ministering to the needs of God's people, protecting, and watching over them. And God's kingdom on this earth continues to grow. Somewhere, light overcame darkness, and love conquered hate. People in increasing numbers are calling upon the name of Jesus and finding help, deliverance, and new life. All over the world today, new voices were heard praising the Lord, and millions of prayers were answered. For more good news in an increasingly dark and lonely world, open your Bible and visit your local church. This is Walter Concrete signing off with the prayer that all *your* news will be good news! Goodnight, folks!

(*Walter exits.*)

74.
Storms of Life

(*Redbeard and Suzanne enter from opposite directions.*)

REDBEARD: Yo ho, lassie!

SUZANNE: Well, shiver me timbers! It's Redbeard the pirate!

REDBEARD: That's right, lassie! The most feared pirate on the seven seas!

SUZANNE: Well, what's new with you, Redbeard?

REDBEARD: I've just written a song—that's what's new with me! You want to hear it?

SUZANNE: No ....

REDBEARD: Then how would you like me to call Jaws and have you walk the plank?

SUZANNE: I was only kidding! Can't you take a joke? Of course I'd like to hear it! How does it go?

REDBEARD: It goes like this! (*He clears his throat and starts singing.*) "Oh ... He went out to sea and he never came back! He went out to sea and he never came back! He took a wrong turn and he never came back! Ha, ha-ha-ha, ha-ha-ho!" (*Laughs.*) How'd you like it?

SUZANNE: What kind of a song was *that*?

REDBEARD: It's a pirate song!

SUZANNE: Well, it's terrible! "He went out to sea and he never came back"—that's terrible!

REDBEARD: Well, what'd you expect? I'm not exactly Michael Jackson!

SUZANNE: That song of yours reminds me of an old saying. Have you ever heard the old saying that says, "Red sky at morning, sailor take warning. Red sky at night, sailor's delight"?

REDBEARD: Aye, lassie! Every sailor knows that one! And many a sailor has ignored the sky, going out to sea only to be caught in a storm—some of them never coming back!

SUZANNE: I was just reading a story in the Bible about a storm at sea—in Mark, the fourth chapter. Jesus and his disciples were sailing across the Sea of Galilee when night fell. (*She recites,*) "And while Jesus slept there arose a great storm...."

(*We hear the sound of a storm.*)

REDBEARD: They're in trouble now!

SUZANNE: "The wind began to blow violently; huge waves arose slamming against the ship, tossing it back and forth...."

REDBEARD: Please, lassie, you're making me seasick!

SUZANNE: "Water started filling the ship—and everyone thought it was going to sink. So the disciples ran and awoke Jesus—to warn Him. But instead of being frightened, Jesus stood in the bow and *spoke* to the wind and the sea saying, 'Peace, be still!' And *immediately* the wind stopped, and the sea grew still. (*The storm sounds cease.*) And there was peace and calm. And the disciples were amazed that even the storm had to obey the Lord Jesus...." What do you think of that?

REDBEARD: I could have used the Lord on a few of my voyages!

SUZANNE: I think we could all use the Lord during the storms of life.

REDBEARD: Aye, lassie. Well, I'll see you later.

SUZANNE: Where you going?

REDBEARD: I'm off to compose another sea chantey! (*Singing.*) "Sixteen men on a dead man's chest ... Yo-ho-ho and a bottle of pop!"

(*Redbeard exits.*)

SUZANNE: And I think I'm off to buy some earplugs!

(*Suzanne exits.*)

75.
Jonah

REDBEARD: Arrrr! Prepare to weigh anchor and set sail!

(Jonah enters)

JONAH: Hold it! Wait! Hold the ship!

REDBEARD: Arrrr! Who are you?

JONAH: My name's Jonah.

REDBEARD: What do you want?

JONAH: I need you to take me somewhere.

REDBEARD: I don't know—I don't normally take passengers.

JONAH: But I'll pay the fare! Whatever it costs.

REDBEARD: In that case . . . where do you want to go?

JONAH: Do you know where Nineveh is?

REDBEARD: Yeah, I know where that is.

JONAH: Well, I *don't* want to go there.

REDBEARD: Arrrr! I didn't ask you where you *don't* want to go! I asked you where you *do* want to go!

JONAH: Let me think . . . How about . . . Nevada! At least that *sounds* like Nineveh! Maybe that will satisfy the Lord. That's where Las Vegas is—they could really use the Lord there.

REDBEARD: We can't sail to Nevada! It's not on the ocean! Crazy landlubber!

JONAH: How about Hawaii? I could do a great work for the Lord in Hawaii! Maybe that would be good enough.

REDBEARD: What do you mean, work for the Lord? Are you some kind of missionary?

JONAH: Yeah. I'm a missionary and traveling preacher.

REDBEARD: But you don't know where the Lord wants you, is that it?

JONAH: No—I know *exactly* where the Lord wants me. He wants me in Nineveh—that's the problem!

REDBEARD: I don't get it!

JONAH: I can't stand Nineveh! I don't like the people there! They're awful! And the Lord is getting ready to judge them! So He's trying to send me there to give them one more chance.

REDBEARD: So why don't you go?

JONAH: Because! I'm such a great preacher that I know they'll all repent and turn to the Lord!

And when the people turn to the Lord, He's so merciful that He'll forgive them all! And they don't deserve it!

REDBEARD: None of us deserve to be forgiven, matey! But that's the wonderful thing about God—He's much more loving and forgiving than any of us!

JONAH: Believe me, it would be better for everybody if the Lord just wipes out Nineveh.

REDBEARD: Let me get this straight. There's a whole country called Nineveh that's been disobedient to the Lord.

JONAH: That's right.

REDBEARD: They won't do what He's told them to do.

JONAH: That's right.

REDBEARD: And the Lord has told you specifically to go there and show them the error of their ways.

JONAH: That's right.

REDBEARD: But you won't go.

JONAH: That about sums it up.

REDBEARD: Why, you're no better than they are!

JONAH: What?!

REDBEARD: You're being disobedient too!

JONAH: Look, I'm the preacher—not you. You're the captain of this ship. So are you going to take me as a passenger or not?

REDBEARD: You're not going to sail on *this* ship! If the Lord is ready to judge Nineveh, He'll probably punish you too for the same offense! And I don't want to be around when it happens! I have a feeling the Lord is going to make you walk the plank!

JONAH: What?

REDBEARD: In other words, you're about to get into a *whale* of a lot of trouble . . . I'm trying to give you a hint, dummy!

JONAH: Well, if you won't take me on board, I'll just go over to the Love Boat! Out of my way!

(Jonah exits.)

REDBEARD: Arrr! That man has oatmeal for brains! But the Lord knows how to get a person's attention. It'll be Jaws IV! Arrr . . .

(Redbeard exits.)

76.
Love

(*Harold and Martha enter*)
HAROLD (*romantically*): Oh, Martha.
MARTHA: Oh, Harold.
HAROLD: Oh, Martha.
MARTHA: Oh, Harold.
HAROLD: Oh, Martha.
MARTHA: Oh, Harold.
HAROLD: Oh, Martha.
MARTHA: Oh, brother ...
HAROLD: Here we are sailing on the Love Boat at last.
MARTHA: Isn't it romantic, Harold?
HAROLD: Only because you're here, Martha.
MARTHA: Oh, Harold, you say the sweetest things.
HAROLD: Martha, do you love me?
MARTHA: Do I what?!
HAROLD: Do you love me?
MARTHA: Well of course I love you, silly boy. For fifteen years I've been your wife. I've cooked for you, cleaned for you, ironed clothes for you ... what further proof do you need?
HAROLD: Thank you, Martha. That's good to know.
MARTHA: Harold?
HAROLD: Yes, Martha?
MARTHA: Do you love *me*?
HAROLD: Martha! For fifteen years I've worked for you, provided for you, mowed the lawn for you, taken out the garbage for you ... what further proof do you need?
MARTHA: But, Harold, what is love? Is it just *working* for one another?
HAROLD: Well, no, it's more than that ... I think.
MARTHA: Then, what is love?
HAROLD: Well, love is ... that gooey feeling you get down in your tummy.
MARTHA: What?! What kind of an answer is that?
HAROLD: It's the best I can do.
(*Redbeard enters.*)
REDBEARD: Ahoy there, mateys! Arrrr, what a beautiful day to set sail! It warms me heart.

HAROLD: Who are you?
REDBEARD: I'm Captain Redbeard. I'm the captain of this here ship!
MARTHA: *You're* the captain of the Love Boat?
REDBEARD: I'm just filling in. The regular captain's taking a vacation on Fantasy Island.
(*A man pops up.*)
MAN: It's dee plane! It's dee plane!
(*The man exits.*)
REDBEARD: Get away from me, you weirdo! Arrrr. We picked him up when we dropped the captain off.
HAROLD: Perhaps you could help us, Captain. Could you tell us what love is?
MARTHA: Don't be ridiculous, Harold. What would he know about love?
REDBEARD: Avast there, matey! I know all about love! God is love! He invented it! It's His very nature. And if we live in God, we'll live in love—and love one another as we should. God loves everyone, and so should we.
HAROLD: Oh, Martha, he's right.
REDBEARD: Well, mateys, I've got to be off now. I've got to hoist the jabbers and swab the poop deck—and all the rest of that sailing stuff. See you later!
(*Redbeard exits.*)
HAROLD: Goodbye, Captain. (*To Martha*): What an interesting fellow.
MARTHA: Oh, Harold, now we know what love is.
HAROLD: Yes, Martha. God is love. All love comes from Him.
MARTHA: Harold, as we sail through life, will you be with me through thick and thin?
HAROLD: Yes, Martha. But speaking of through thick and thin—when are you going on that diet you've been talking about?
MARTHA: Diet!!! I'll diet you! Hiiiiyaaaaaa!
(*She hits him. We hear a gong. Martha then exits.*)
HAROLD: Oh, Martha ....
(*Harold sinks out of sight.*)

Resource Guide

Puppets

Son Rise Puppet Company
P.O. Box 5091—FCPD, Salem, OR 97304
(Send 50¢ for catalog.)

Puppets That Praise
8455 Oak Street
Newburgh, IN 47630
(Custom-made puppets of excellent quality. No catalog available.)

Sydney the Squirrel Puppet
Standard Publishing, Order #3685, ($6.95) Camel-colored fur, 10½" tall hand puppet with lifelike eyes and a big, toothy grin. Sports a green bow tie.
800-543-1353, in OH, 800-582-1385

From John, With Love
B5, $6.95 Twelve-inch hand puppet of John comes with several scripts to share experiences from his Gospel of love.

Scripts from Standard Publishing

Puppet plays for "New Creatures" #R3353
($4.95) Directions and patterns for making the five puppets used in these thirteen clever scripts are included in this book.

Puppet Plays—Adventures of Charlie and His Friends #R2762 ($3.95) Thirty-four captivating plays and four games teach Bible stories and speak about such subjects as faith, trust, patience, thanking God, and following Jesus.

Puppet Plays With a Point #R3365 $7.95 Step-by-step instructions for making hand puppets with moveable mouths, and sock-puppet animals, directions for making a stage, fourteen original songs with easy-to-learn melodies, piano parts to enhance your presentations, and eighteen scripts for puppeteers of all ages.

Puppets and Scripts

Bible True Audio Visuals
1441 South Busse Road
Mt. Prospect, IL 60056 (*Free catalog.*)

Maher Studios
P.O. Box 420
Littleton, CO 80160
(*Also taped shows, ventriloquist supplies. Free catalog.*)

One Way Street, Inc.
Box 2398
Littleton, CO 80160 (*Also puppet stage plans, newsletter. Send $1.00 for catalog.*)

Puppet Productions Inc.
P.O. Box 82008
San Diego, CA 92138
(*Also taped shows. Free catalog.*)

Puppet Pals
Dept. C 100 Belhaven Dr.
Los Gatos, CA 95030
(*Also taped shows. Free catalog.*)

Music and Sound Effects

The following sources have music and sound effects available with a one-time purchase agreement. No needle-drop fees are charged. You may therefore duplicate the music and effects on your own master tracks whenever you like. All of the following sources will send you a free brochure and sample tape or album of their music and sound effects.

Creative Support Services
1950 Riverside Drive
Los Angeles, CA 90039
(*Music.*)

Production EFX Library
2325 Girard Ave. S.
Minneapolis, MN 55405 (*Sound effects.*)

Music Masters, Inc.
17 Ponca Trail
St. Louis, MO 63122
(*Music.*)

ZM Squared
903 Edgewood Lane
Cinnaminson, NJ 08077
(*Music and audio visual products.*)

DeWolfe Music Library, Inc.
25 West 45th Street
New York, NY 10036
(*DeWolfe charges a needle-drop fee for the use of their music, but you can buy their sound effects albums outright. I use musical jangles from their "Comedy Effects" album to end all my shows.*)